W9-BGN-504

yogurt

yogurt

SWEET AND SAVORY RECIPES FOR BREAKFAST, LUNCH, AND DINNER

Janet Fletcher

Photographs by Eva Kolenko

TEN SPEED PRESS
Berkeley

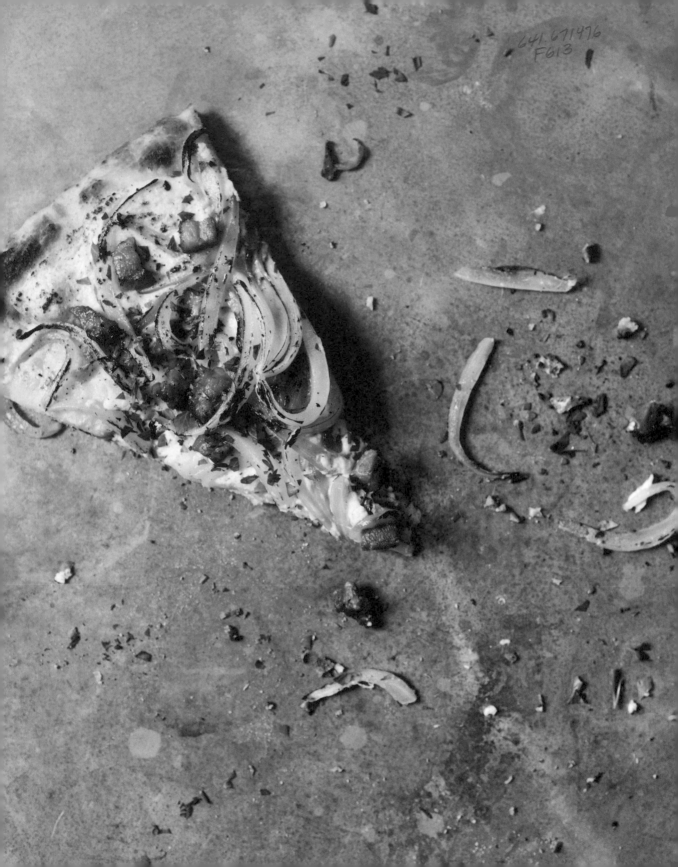

103 Desserts

125 Beverages

Introduction

Drizzled with honey or dolloped on fruit, yogurt is a gift from nature. We humans have refined the recipe, but nature created it and showed us the way. Thousands of years ago—who knows when?—some herder in Central Asia probably left an animal-skin pouch of goat's milk in the sun and came back to find the milk thickened and sour. It tasted pleasant (we have to presume), it lasted longer than fresh milk, and it was more digestible. Eventually, some resourceful goatherds realized they didn't have to wait for nature to intervene: they could instigate the milk's transformation themselves. A little yogurt stirred into fresh milk would produce more yogurt.

Thick and creamy, wholesome and health-promoting, yogurt nourishes us from daybreak to bedtime. A bowl of yogurt, peaches, and granola to start the day . . . an asparagus frittata with yogurt at lunch . . . lamb meatballs in a spicy yogurt sauce for dinner. Yogurt tantalizes us with its possibilities, with all the directions it can go. Sweet or savory? In a strawberry smoothie or stirred into soup? With blueberries and maple syrup . . . or with cucumbers, walnuts, and mint?

As a cook, I love where yogurt has taken me. It has sent me diving into Indian cookbooks to learn more about raitas, the spicy yogurt salads fragrant with mustard seed and cumin. I've explored Turkey—on the ground and in books—and fallen in love with its yogurt salads, similar to raitas but totally different in seasoning. Garlic, dill, and mint are the Turkish signature, ever-present in these salads and in Turkey's aromatic, yogurt-thickened soups.

Friends from India, Turkey, Greece, and Lebanon have introduced me to other traditional yogurt dishes: charcoal-grilled souvlaki on a bed of yogurt with homemade flatbread; braised lamb shoulder with artichokes and yogurt; variations on Greece's cucumber tzatziki; and the seductive *shrikhand*, an Indian yogurt dessert scented with cardamom and saffron. I've also been influenced by the contemporary, stylish suggestions for enjoying fresh yogurt proposed by American yogurt producers.

At some point, as enthusiastic cooks always do, I began to develop my own ways of using yogurt that reflect my taste and California sensibilities. I've never cared much for contemporary fusion food, the sort of cooking that ignores traditional foodways and the flavor combinations that have evolved over centuries. But I'm all in favor of building on tradition and using familiar dishes as a bridge to new taste experiences. An Indian cook might never pair a red-onion raita with a grilled hanger steak, but I consider that marriage highly successful (page 77). Italians don't typically put yogurt cheese in a frittata, but creamy dollops in an asparagus frittata seem to me an enhancement (page 101). In Lebanon, land of *za'atar* (the Middle Eastern spice blend), I doubt that many people know farro, but a sprinkle of *za'atar* invigorates a farro salad with summer vegetables and yogurt (page 48).

A Little History

Yogurt has nourished civilizations since perhaps 5000 BCE. Food historians surmise that it originated in Central Asia, almost surely by happenstance when ambient strains of *Lactobacillus delbrueckii* subspecies *bulgaricus* and *Streptococcus thermophilus* thickened and soured fresh milk. These bacteria will ferment any mammal's milk—cow, goat, sheep, camel, yak, mare, water buffalo—so yogurt would have been of tremendous nutritional value to early pastoral peoples. Fresh milk, which might spoil in hot climates in just a few hours, could safely nourish people for days if encouraged to acidify into yogurt. By producing lactic acid and lowering the milk's pH, the "good" bacteria in yogurt make life difficult for spoilage bacteria and pathogens. Drained and salted, yogurt lasts even longer, as the ancients surely discovered.

From Central Asia, yogurt likely passed into present-day Iran, then west to Turkey and the Balkans, east to Afghanistan, and south to Pakistan and India. A line drawn from Belgrade to Baghdad to Bangalore would loosely trace the arc of yogurt eaters before recent times. The Bible refers to Abraham serving curds and milk to guests. Was that yogurt? Pliny the Elder wrote about nomadic tribes that knew how to thicken milk into a pleasantly acidic curd. Was that yogurt? According to food historian Clifford Wright, the first written description of what was unequivocally yogurt appears in an eleventh-century dictionary compiled during the Seljuk reign in the Middle East.

The English word *yogurt* is Turkish in origin, and etymologists believe the Turkish word derives from the root *yog*, meaning "to condense or thicken." The Turks helped spread yogurt to western Europe, but it was a Russian microbiologist, Ilya Mechnikov, who really sparked today's widespread enthusiasm for yogurt.

The 1908 Nobel Prize winner in medicine, Mechnikov became intrigued by the long lives of Bulgarians and thought their high yogurt consumption might play a role. During his years at the Pasteur Institute in Paris, he developed a theory that lactic acid bacteria in the gut could help prolong life by combating toxic bacteria—a notion that underlies probiotics research today. Mechnikov surmised that we could, through diet, modify our intestinal flora, replacing harmful microbes with beneficial ones.

Mechnikov's work caught the attention of Isaac Carasso, a Greek who had moved to Spain in 1912. Carasso was struck by how many Spanish children suffered from intestinal illnesses. Reading Mechnikov and recalling that people in the Balkans ate yogurt for digestive maladies, he opened a small plant to make yogurt in Barcelona. The year was 1919, and yogurt was so little known in Spain that Carasso sold it through pharmacies as medicine. He named the business Danone, after his son Daniel.

Daniel Carasso, who studied business, picked up where his father left off. He introduced Danone to France, selling it in dairy stores. Eventually the French embraced it, but then World War II intervened. Fleeing the Nazis, Carasso immigrated to the United States in 1941, bringing his yogurt expertise with him. He soon found partners and began manufacturing in the Bronx in 1942, packaging plain yogurt in half-pint glass bottles. For his new customers, he Americanized the business name, rebranding as Dannon. Over the course of his lifetime—he died in 2009 at the age of 103—yogurt transitioned from obscure ethnic food to big business.

A Little Science

The spontaneous fermentation that produced the first yogurt has evolved into a carefully controlled and well-understood process. Even so, commercial yogurts vary noticeably from one brand to another. These differences reflect how each manufacturer handles the milk before culturing, and the choice of cultures, fermentation temperature and duration, target acidity, and technique.

Unless they operate on a small scale, most manufacturers adjust their milk to hit target fat and protein ratios so they can achieve consistent results. Even if making full-fat yogurt, they may blend skim milk and cream with whole milk to arrive at the precise fat percentage they want. Many manufacturers add nonfat dry milk or powdered milk protein to raise the solids without adding fat; more solids (mainly protein) produce a thicker and more stable yogurt, less likely to release whey over time. Some use reverse osmosis to remove water from the milk, a method of raising the percentage of solids without using dry milk. Many add stabilizers, such as gelatin, tapioca starch, or pectin (see page 6), before the milk is pasteurized. For Greek yogurt, manufacturers use a variety of approaches to concentrate the milk before culturing it (see page 5), or they may centrifuge it after fermentation to remove whey.

By law, commercial yogurt in the United States must be made with pasteurized milk. Pasteurization kills pathogens, such as *Listeria* and *Salmonella*. But there are other reasons to pasteurize. By lowering the milk's bacterial count, pasteurization clears the way for the cultures to do their work, unimpeded by competing bacteria. And the high temperatures typically used to pasteurize milk for yogurt—higher than for cheese milk—denature whey proteins. As a result, more of those proteins become part of the gel, making the yogurt thicker and more stable.

Following pasteurization and, in most cases, homogenization, the milk is cooled to the desired inoculation temperature, typically between 108°F and 114°F. The cultures are added and fermentation begins as the bacteria begin to consume the milk sugar (lactose) and produce lactic acid.

Yogurt culture blends are proprietary. Many manufacturers reveal the different bacteria they use—they even list them on the ingredients label—but not the specific strains or the ratios. *Streptococcus thermophilus* (ST) and *Lactobacillus delbrueckii* subsp. *bulgaricus* (LB) are starter cultures and they are mandatory, part of the federal government's standard for yogurt.

ST bacteria start the ball rolling. They grow faster than LB in the early stage, and are responsible for the initial rise in acidity and drop in pH from about 6.5 to 5.0. They lay the foundation for LB to grow. LB bacteria work symbiotically with ST. Either bacterium would ferment milk, but the two stimulate each other and grow faster together. LB continues the acid production when ST slows, driving the pH down further to an end point around 4.4.

Choosing Yogurt

The proliferating yogurt selection at the market is enough to unnerve any consumer. How do you make the right choice from a display that includes more brands every time you shop? Those tubs and jars all contain yogurt, but the differences can be pronounced. The following questions can help you wade through the options. Once you understand the choices, you can find yogurt that suits your taste.

PLAIN OR FLAVORED?

I personally buy only plain, unflavored yogurt, and all the recipes in this book use plain yogurt. Why let a manufacturer sweeten your yogurt when you can easily sweeten it to taste? Start with plain yogurt and you can add brown sugar, date sugar, maple syrup, agave nectar, homemade jam, or local wildflower honey. Why buy strawberry yogurt with mushy berries when you can stir in fresh berries from the farmers' market—a tastier and more nutritious alternative? Be your own flavor boss and go for the plain.

Study the ingredients label on flavored yogurts. Most brands include sweeteners, stabilizers, unidentified "natural flavorings," and colorants. These yogurts taste more like pudding to me than like the pure cultured milk that inspired them.

Plain yogurt, with its lactic tang, may be an acquired taste for some. But like the wine drinker who eventually transitions from sweet blush wines to more complex reds, people who cultivate a taste for plain yogurt soon find that most flavored yogurts taste too sweet.

Even plain yogurt varies considerably from one brand to another. Two manufacturers may use the same cultures but in different proportions, or they may use different bacterial strains. Most yogurt manufacturers have a "house style," so you can

expect a similar texture and taste from a brand every time. Some brands are intentionally tarter or thinner than others—that's their signature—so play the field to find a style you like.

COW, GOAT, OR SHEEP?

Cow's-milk yogurt dominates the market in the United States, and most of the prominent national brands use cow's milk. But a handful of creameries, such as Redwood Hill Farms in California, distribute goat's-milk yogurt nationally, and numerous regional creameries produce it. Many consumers find goat's-milk yogurt more digestible. Goat's-milk has smaller fat globules than cow's milk, so our digestive tract breaks down the fat more easily. Some people simply prefer the lemony taste of goat's-milk yogurt over the more buttery cow's-milk type, while some choose goat yogurt because they are allergic to cow's milk.

Sheep's-milk yogurt, the standard in Greece and Turkey, has limited availability in the United States because dairy sheep remain scarce. Their milk is much higher in fat than cow's or goat's milk, giving sheep's-milk yogurt an especially rich and buttery taste. Because of the milk's scarcity and the high demand for it from artisanal cheese makers, sheep's-milk yogurt tends to be expensive. When you find it, consider treating yourself to a splurge.

You can use cow's-milk, goat's-milk, or sheep's-milk yogurt interchangeably in the recipes in this book. More important than the animal source is the fat content.

WHOLE MILK, LOW-FAT, OR NONFAT?

Most of the dishes in this book can be made with low-fat yogurt, but when I specify whole-milk (full-fat) yogurt, it's because I believe a good outcome depends on it. Whole-milk yogurt is richer, smoother, and fuller in body. Reduced-fat yogurt tends to be tangier, chalkier, and less silky and luscious. No surprise there. Milk fat contributes buttery notes and mouthfeel. It balances yogurt's acidity in the way that cream softens coffee. But for people accustomed to nonfat or low-fat yogurt, whole-milk yogurt may seem *too* rich and palate-coating, and not lively enough.

From the preponderance of low-fat and nonfat yogurts in markets, I know that whole-milk yogurt is not the popular choice. Even so, I hope you will consider it for these recipes unless you must reduce dietary fat. Almost any dish will taste better if made with whole-milk yogurt, and the calorie difference per serving is minimal. In a recipe for four that calls for one cup of yogurt, choosing a whole-milk product over nonfat raises the calorie count by about 50. Divided four ways, that's a modest investment in better texture and taste.

What's more, several studies published in peer-reviewed journals have found a seeming paradox: whole-milk dairy consumption was associated with a *lower* risk of obesity. Researchers theorize that full-fat dairy products satisfy us more quickly, so we eat less of them; or possibly milk fat alters our metabolism in a way that keeps our bodies from storing the fat.

GREEK OR REGULAR?

In traditional yogurt-eating countries such as Greece and Turkey, yogurt prepared at home is often drained through a cloth for an hour or more after the yogurt sets (see page 23). Draining removes whey and yields a velvety, thick yogurt that keeps longer. But on a commercial scale, draining in this manner isn't practical or considered hygienic. To produce the thick yogurt that they label as Greek, many manufacturers use filtration to concentrate the milk before culturing it, or a centrifuge to eliminate whey

after fermentation. Some producers of Greek yogurt add cornstarch or powdered milk protein or whey protein and don't drain the product at all. The boom in sales for Greek yogurt has driven manufacturers to explore new ways to make it without having to invest in expensive equipment. As a result, Greek yogurts vary a lot in texture.

A few desserts in this book, such as panna cotta (page 116) and yogurt sorbet (page 121), benefit from the richness and body of Greek yogurt. But for most of these recipes, many commercial Greek yogurts are too thick, stiff, and buttery, almost like sour cream. (The lovely Straus Family Creamery Greek yogurt is a notable West Coast exception.) The softer texture of plain yogurt or home-drained yogurt (page 22) is more appealing, especially in salads. With home-drained yogurt, you decide how long to drain and, consequently, you control the yogurt's eventual thickness.

"LIVE ACTIVE CULTURES" OR "HEAT-TREATED AFTER CULTURING"?

To enjoy yogurt's purported benefits for digestive health (see page 7), look for a brand with live active cultures. If the label doesn't list live active cultures, put the container back. The yogurt was likely pasteurized or heat-treated to extend its shelf life, killing all or most of the probiotics (health-promoting bacteria) added to the milk. Yogurts with live active cultures are made with pasteurized milk, but the milk is cultured *after* pasteurization.

Also, if you want to use store-bought yogurt as a starter for a homemade batch, you must choose a yogurt with live active cultures. Without live cultures, the yogurt won't perform as a starter.

DO MORE CULTURES MAKE BETTER YOGURT?

If only two cultures are needed to make yogurt—
Lactobacillus delbrueckii subsp. *bulgaricus* and
Streptococcus thermophilus—why the long list of
Latin names on some yogurt containers? Other
bacteria (such as *Bifidobacterium lactis*, *Lactobacillus
acidophilus*, *L. casei*, and *L. rhamnosus*) are often
added to yogurt as probiotics, for the presumed
health benefits (see page 7). If yogurt's probiotic
qualities are important to you, then seek out a brand
with these probiotic cultures and make sure the label
says "live active cultures."

WHAT ABOUT STABILIZERS?

Many yogurt manufacturers rely on stabilizers
such as pectin and tapioca starch to create a firmer,
sturdier texture. Stabilizers also prevent "wheying
off," the release of milky whey that happens over
time, especially in a partially consumed container.
These stabilizers are perfectly safe, natural, and
tasteless, but I dislike the texture they produce.
Yogurts made with stabilizers often seem too stiff
or gelatinous to me.

My favorite yogurts contain nothing but milk and
live active cultures—no pectin, gelatin, starches, or
gums. That said, almost all commercial goat yogurt
contains stabilizers because the yogurt would be
unacceptably thin and fragile without them. A few
producers use reverse osmosis or microfiltration to
remove water from goat's milk before culturing,
which allows them to produce a yogurt that doesn't
need stabilizing.

Stabilized plain yogurt should work in these recipes,
and in some markets, it may be your only option.
If you don't have a ready source of nonstabilized
yogurt, consider making your own so you can
experience its delicate, supple texture.

HOW TO ENHANCE YOGURT'S LONGEVITY

Yogurt will stay fresh in the refrigerator for
at least three weeks if you pay attention to
sanitation. If you're sloppy about it, the flavor
may change noticeably in seven to ten days.
Here are some pointers for extending the
yogurt's refrigerated life:

- Take what you need from the yogurt
  container, and then immediately put it
  back in the fridge. Don't let the container
  sit out on the kitchen counter while you're
  having breakfast.

- Always use a clean spoon in the yogurt
  container. Don't take another helping with
  a spoon you've eaten with or you will
  introduce bacteria. This won't make the
  yogurt unsafe to eat, but it could hasten
  its decline.

- Drain your yogurt (see page 22) for at least
  one hour. Removing whey, which contains
  lactose, slows bacteria by taking away
  their food.

Yogurt & Your Health

I eat and cook with yogurt because I love the taste; any health benefits are a bonus. But evidence for those benefits keeps mounting as nutrition researchers and epidemiologists dig deeper. While modern science, with its peer-reviewed research, rigorously examines the case for eating yogurt, anecdotal evidence of yogurt's role in well-being has circulated for centuries.

Our ancestors used yogurt as a sunscreen, a skin cream, a sleep aid, and a treatment for impotence. Although we no longer look to yogurt for those functions, some of the properties the ancients attributed to yogurt remain a subject of study. Galen, the second-century Greek physician and influential medical scholar, believed that yogurt improved digestion. Fourteen centuries later, a Turkish doctor summoned to treat King Francis I of France reportedly repaired the royal intestines with yogurt. The doctor brought a flock of sheep with him from Constantinople so he could concoct the prescription on the spot. Did yogurt really cure the king? We'll never know, but certainly yogurt's contribution to digestive health has credence today.

Like the milk it comes from, plain yogurt is a good source of calcium, protein, riboflavin, phosphorus, vitamin B12, and vitamin D. But yogurt differs from milk in two key ways that may confer additional health benefits: it typically (not always) contains less lactose than milk, and many brands contain live active cultures. Let's look more closely at both of these features and their possible impact on health.

REDUCED LACTOSE

Many people who can't consume fresh milk without gastric distress find yogurt more digestible. Yogurt is not lactose-free, but it usually has less lactose than milk because the bacteria in the culture have converted some of the milk's lactose into lactic acid.

These bacteria slow down before they ferment all the lactose, inhibited by yogurt's high acidity and by refrigeration. Consequently, most yogurts still have significant lactose—approximately 8 grams per cup compared to 12 grams per cup for milk. Drained or Greek yogurt typically has slightly less lactose because draining removes whey, where a lot of the unfermented sugar resides.

You might imagine that yogurt *always* contains less lactose than milk, but for some yogurt that's not so. Many manufacturers add nonfat dry milk to the milk used for yogurt, a technique for increasing the protein and improving the body, especially in reduced-fat yogurt. But the dry milk also boosts lactose, so that even after fermentation, the yogurt may have a lactose content comparable to that of milk.

Lactose-sensitive people differ in how much lactose they can tolerate. If you have trouble digesting milk sugar, choose yogurt brands without nonfat dry milk (if used, it will be a listed ingredient) and with relatively few grams of sugar. If you make your own yogurt by my method (see pages 11–20), omit the nonfat dry milk.

LIVE ACTIVE CULTURES

Scientists are a long way from understanding probiotic bacteria. Which species and strains are probiotic? What do these beneficial microbes do for us, and how do they do it? What "dose" of probiotic bacteria will be therapeutic? And do probiotic supplements provide the same health benefits as yogurt? With probiotics, researchers have more questions than answers. Certainly the health claims made for yogurt and its probiotic bacteria have occasionally outraced the science.

The yogurt picture is especially complicated because manufacturers use different cultures;

even two manufacturers that use the same bacteria may choose different strains of those bacteria. And any health benefits from a particular strain may apply only to that strain. So while the research into probiotics is lively and promising, study results don't translate easily into dietary recommendations. The research is suggestive, but not conclusive.

The two bacteria common to every yogurt—*Lactobacillus delbrueckii* subsp. *bulgaricus* and *Streptococcus thermophilus*—are the fermentation workforce. They do the job of breaking down the lactose, producing lactic acid, and coagulating the milk. The other bacteria commonly found in yogurt cultures—*Lactobacillus acidophilus, L. casei, L. rhamnosus,* and *Bifidobacterium lactis*—are included largely as probiotics, though *L. acidophilus* does contribute some tartness.

With growing confidence, scientists say that the probiotic bacteria in yogurt with live active cultures can minimize the unpleasant side effects, particularly diarrhea, of antibiotics use. Probiotics appear to protect us against upper respiratory tract infections, making our colds fewer and shorter. There's some evidence that probiotics can help people with digestive issues like constipation and irritable bowel syndrome. And infants born to women who consume probiotics before delivery have a lower incidence of dermatitis. Researchers continue to find positive correlations between probiotics and a healthy digestive system, healthy immune system, and healthy metabolism—all subjects of ongoing study.

Whether the probiotics in yogurt function better than probiotic supplements remains to be proved. But why resort to pills when you can enjoy much more delicious "medicine" in a bowl of yogurt?

To enjoy the full extent of yogurt's health benefits, choose a yogurt with live active cultures. Yogurt that is heat-treated after culturing—a procedure that prolongs shelf life—contains few or no viable probiotic (health-enhancing) bacteria. If the yogurt contains live active cultures, the label will say so. Homemade yogurt will have live active cultures.

A Note About the Recipes

For a few dishes, I specify whole-milk yogurt; for others, drained or Greek. Sometimes nonfat yogurt will work; for other recipes, I advise against it. Many of these recipes simply call for plain yogurt, with no further detail. Those recipes will work regardless of the type of yogurt you use.

Supermarkets carry so many styles of plain yogurt, of varying fat contents and textures, that it's not easy—or even always possible—to write a recipe that works with all of them. Some brands are soupy, while others are stiff enough to hold a spoon upright. Some are mellow and buttery, while others are bracingly tart. Nonfat and low-fat yogurts are inclined to curdle with even a little heat. Drained and Greek yogurts are likely to be more heat-stable because they are typically less acidic: you can put a dollop on hot soup and not worry that it will break. Greek yogurt has a luscious mouthfeel, but some brands are simply *too* thick and rich for some recipes.

This product variability explains why I often suggest the type of yogurt to use. For some dishes, only drained yogurt, made from store-bought or homemade yogurt, will produce the supple, creamy texture that the finished dish should have. In other instances, the choice isn't crucial and I leave it up to you to decide whether you want the lightness of low-fat yogurt or the silky fullness of whole-milk yogurt.

In my own kitchen, I don't use nonfat yogurt and don't recommend it for any of these recipes, apart from the smoothies. I find most nonfat yogurts too tart—they have no fat to balance the tang—and the texture is often chalky or sandy, not smooth and creamy. The choice is yours, of course, but I think you will be happier with the recipe outcome if you use the type of yogurt that I recommend.

IF THE RECIPE CALLS FOR . . .

PLAIN YOGURT: Whole-milk yogurt is preferred, but low-fat or nonfat will work; Greek yogurt is likely to be too thick.

PLAIN YOGURT (NOT NONFAT): Whole-milk yogurt is preferred but low-fat will work; do not use nonfat. Greek yogurt is likely to be too thick.

PLAIN WHOLE-MILK YOGURT: The dish benefits from the extra richness of whole-milk yogurt. Low-fat, nonfat, and Greek yogurts are not recommended.

PLAIN DRAINED YOGURT: Use homemade or store-bought yogurt drained for about 1 hour as described on page 22; preferably whole-milk but low-fat or nonfat will work; Greek yogurt is likely to be too thick.

PLAIN DRAINED YOGURT OR GREEK YOGURT (NOT NONFAT): Use homemade or store-bought yogurt drained for about 1 hour as described on page 22; preferably whole-milk but low-fat will work; Greek whole-milk or low-fat yogurt will also work.

PLAIN DRAINED WHOLE-MILK YOGURT OR GREEK WHOLE-MILK YOGURT: The recipe benefits from the extra richness of whole milk. Low-fat and nonfat yogurts are not recommended.

Making Yogurt at Home

I love opening my refrigerator and seeing a quart jar of just-made yogurt, full of possibilities. The jar never stays full for long. Yogurt is everyday fare at my house, and being without it would be like running out of coffee. Not going to happen. I like a dollop on fruit in the morning, with a dusting of brown sugar. Or for lunch, I'll improvise a smoothie with yogurt, frozen bananas, and whatever fresh fruit is at hand. At dinnertime, I'll explore the vegetable bin, and even if my dig turns up nothing but a bunch of spinach or a handful of carrots, I'll have the makings of a tasty yogurt salad.

I buy a lot of yogurt, but I make even more. It saves money, and I enjoy the magic. Fresh fluid milk goes into a jar and comes out firm. Even now, after years of making yogurt at home, the outcome still seems like a miracle.

FIVE STEPS TO
HOMEMADE YOGURT

Heat milk to
180°F to 195°F.

Cool milk to 115°F.

Inoculate with
chosen culture.

Incubate at 108°F
(plus or minus a few degrees)
until set.

Refrigerate to firm.

Optional: Drain for
extra thickness and life span.

Until modern times, yogurt was always made at home, without pasteurized milk, instant-read thermometers, or electric yogurt makers. Even today, many people remember their mother or grandmother making yogurt with only a saucepan, a bowl, and a blanket. Women would put drops of scalded milk on their wrist to know if the milk had cooled enough to add the culture. Some old-timers say they knew the milk was ready when they could comfortably put their finger in it and count to ten. Lacking an electric appliance to keep the fermenting milk warm and happy, people would swaddle their yogurt bowl in blankets and put it by the woodstove.

Surely, under these circumstances, batches occasionally went awry. Ambient bacteria (perhaps from that dipping finger) infected the milk and produced off flavors. Or the incubating milk got too cold and the culture stalled or refused to work at all. In yesteryear's drafty houses, it must have taken some effort to keep the fermenting milk warm, in the temperature range that the bacteria like (roughly 105°F to 115°F).

Today's electric yogurt appliances provide a steady, warm incubation environment, eliminating the guesswork. Some allow you to set the incubation temperature you desire, and to adjust it during fermentation if you like. Others are engineered to maintain a suitable temperature; you need only plug them in.

If you live in an urban or suburban community, you probably have an abundance of tasty commercial yogurts available to you. Even so, you may want to consider making yogurt on occasion, for the savings it affords and the pleasure that comes from something homemade. If you live where food choices are fewer, making yogurt at home may be your only regular opportunity to enjoy traditional yogurt, produced with nothing but milk and cultures.

To make yogurt at home, you need milk, a starter culture, and an incubation method. You have many options for each, and your choices will affect your results.

Choosing Milk

Always start with fresh milk from an unopened container. You can make yogurt with nonfat, low-fat, or whole milk; and with milk from cows, goats, or sheep. (Fortunate is the person with access to sheep's milk. It is exceptionally high in fat and protein and makes luscious yogurt.) I use whole milk because I like the richer flavor and body that fat provides. The higher the milk fat, the creamier and richer the yogurt feels in your mouth. You can even add some half-and-half or cream for extra-rich yogurt—if you intend to use it for dessert, perhaps. Start with 10 percent half-and-half or cream to 90 percent milk and see if you like the results.

But while full-fat milk yields yogurt that makes a voluptuous impression, it is largely protein that makes yogurt thick. If you choose to use reduced-fat milk (nonfat or low-fat), I recommend adding instant nonfat dry milk in the ratio of two tablespoons per quart of milk. The dry milk boosts the solids content (mostly protein) in your milk base, yielding firmer, thicker yogurt and partly compensating for the lack of fat. A little instant nonfat dry milk even makes whole-milk yogurt firmer and more satisfying, so I almost always add it. I prefer instant dry milk, which dissolves readily. Regular dry milk works, too, but it takes a lot of whisking to get it to dissolve in fluid milk. Boosting the solids in this way is comparable to what commercial yogurt makers do when they concentrate the milk with reverse osmosis (see page 3) before culturing.

Goat's milk has fewer solids than cow's milk, so it yields a more delicate and thinner yogurt. (That's why most goat-yogurt manufacturers add stabilizers.) You can make a thicker yogurt from goat's milk by whisking in two tablespoons instant nonfat dry milk per quart of milk. Dry cow's milk is fine to use—unless you are allergic to it, of course. Dry goat's milk is available from online sources, but it is expensive.

You can use homogenized or nonhomogenized milk for yogurt, but the latter will yield yogurt with a thin layer of cream on the top. Just stir it in when you eat it. Do not use ultra-pasteurized (UHT) milk, which is not suited to culturing.

Choosing a Starter

Until modern times—and still today in many households—yogurt was typically homemade, produced from milk cultured with a little yogurt from the previous batch. Just as with a sourdough starter for bread, each batch of yogurt should contain enough live bacteria to launch the next fermentation. Food writer Paula Wolfert says that she used to tell her children that they could eat as much of the yogurt in the fridge as they liked, as long as they didn't eat it all. She needed some to inoculate the next batch.

The long-perpetuated yogurt culture is as precious in some households as the sourdough-bread starter is in others. Harold McGee, who writes on the science of food, mentions the resourceful immigrants' tactic of dipping a cloth in homemade yogurt and letting it dry in order to transport that beloved taste to their new home. Did those dormant bacteria in the cloth survive the move across oceans and continents, springing to life again in a pot of warm milk? Possibly. Did they yield a yogurt in California like the yogurt they made in Pakistan? Maybe not, but the effort suggests how much cultural importance we attach to our most fundamental culinary ingredients.

Today, we have three ways to culture milk for yogurt: with store-bought yogurt containing live active bacteria; with homemade yogurt; or with a purchased dried culture. All three processes rely on the same two bacteria—*Lactobacillus delbrueckii* subsp. *bulgaricus* and *Streptococcus thermophilus*—to transform fluid milk into spoonable yogurt.

STORE-BOUGHT YOGURT

For your starter, purchase plain yogurt with live active bacteria. Fruit yogurt can have undesirable yeasts and bacteria that may outcompete the starter culture. You can use cow's-milk yogurt to inoculate goat's milk, if you like, and vice versa. What's important is the presence of live active cultures. If you use store-bought yogurt as a starter culture, use a freshly opened container to be sure you are inoculating your milk with only desirable bacteria. A partially used container may contain ambient bacteria from being left open on the breakfast table, or bacteria from a not-so-clean serving spoon.

Needless to say, choose a brand that you like. Some yogurts are tangier, some more mellow—a reflection of the culture "cocktail" that the manufacturer uses. If you use a tangy store-bought yogurt for a starter, your yogurt will likely be tangy, too. Even an unopened container of commercial yogurt becomes slightly more tart over time, so check the expiration date on the container.

HOMEMADE YOGURT

Using homemade yogurt as a starter culture has a lot of appeal because it costs nothing and provides the satisfaction of keeping a starter going. However, you should be aware of the challenges. Yogurt cultures evolve over time, as the bacteria in them grow and die at different rates. Consequently, yogurt made by this subculturing method also evolves over time and may eventually become thinner, tarter, or less stable than you would like. In that event, you may need to start over with store-bought yogurt or a purchased dried culture.

To maintain the vigor and purity of your starter culture, make yogurt often—at least once a week. Homemade yogurt that is less than a week old should have the right balance of bacteria to serve as a starter.

DRIED CULTURE

If you use purchased dried culture (see Resources, page 135), also called yogurt starter, follow the manufacturer's directions. Keep unused culture in the freezer, where it should remain viable for up to one year.

More culture is not better. Using more starter culture than a recipe calls for will not produce a faster set or a thicker yogurt. In fact, the opposite is more likely. The milk may not contain enough lactose to "feed" all the bacteria, and they may die before they coagulate the milk.

YOGURT TOO TART?

If your yogurt is too acidic, it's likely that your culture is out of balance. A freeze-dried culture should perform consistently over time, but if you are using homemade yogurt as your starter, you may notice batches becoming progressively tarter. That's a sign that *Lactobacillus bulgaricus* is dominating your yogurt and possibly inhibiting the growth of probiotic bacteria like *L. acidophilus*. To restore the equilibrium, use a store-bought yogurt or a freeze-dried culture to inoculate your next batch.

Choosing an Incubation Method

Yogurt bacteria tolerate a range of roughly 105°F to 115°F. A temperature of 118°F or higher will kill most cultures. If the incubation temperature falls below 105°F, the culture will produce more polysaccharides and the yogurt will likely be slimy or "ropy" or may not set at all.

Your challenge as a home yogurt-maker is coddling the culture, keeping it in the desired range for the several hours it takes to do its job. Know where and how you are going to incubate the yogurt before you start, and test to make sure you can maintain temperature. To test, fill a jar with water at 115°F and "incubate" it in your chosen manner as if it were cultured milk, taking its temperature with an instant-read thermometer every hour or so.

If you are using a yogurt-making appliance, follow the manufacturer's directions. Before you use it for the first time, and occasionally thereafter, verify the incubation temperature using a jar or two of water, as described above. Of course, if the machine is producing yogurt reliably for you, you don't need to question its thermostat. But if you are having trouble getting batches to set, it could be because the device is malfunctioning.

In the days when I was merely an occasional yogurt consumer, my five-cup electric maker suited me fine. The machine never failed to set the milk in its little glass cups, and although the yogurt was often a tad grainy on the bottom of the cup—where the heat was higher—the convenience more than compensated for that last less-than-perfect spoonful.

But I am now a yogurt enthusiast, inclined to eat it daily and cook with it often. I need more volume than these small appliances produce, so I typically culture a half-gallon of milk at a time in two quart jars. If you're an avid consumer, too, you can purchase a yogurt-making appliance that accommodates quart jars, or you can make yogurt the old-fashioned way, by locating or creating a consistently warm incubation environment (see page 17).

I have had excellent results with the Brød & Taylor folding proofer (see Resources, page 135). This electric appliance, originally intended for bread proofing, works splendidly for yogurt, too. It isn't inexpensive, but it has several useful features. You can set its thermostat to a precise temperature (I use 110°F for yogurt), and you can alter that temperature during the fermentation. On the company's website, you

PURCHASING A
YOGURT MAKER

You don't need an electric yogurt appliance to make yogurt at home. But if you struggle to maintain a stable incubating temperature, you may find a machine worth the investment. Two key features to consider before you buy:

CAPACITY: How much yogurt can the machine make at once, and what size jars does it accommodate? The machines that hold only a few six-ounce jars may not make enough volume for your needs if you're an avid consumer.

CONTROLS: Does the device have a timer so that you can set it to incubate for a desired length of time? Does it have an automatic shutoff feature so that you don't have to be at home to turn it off? Some machines have automatic cooling, which might be desirable. Does it a have a variable thermostat that you control so you can set the incubation temperature you prefer? And how reliably does it maintain incubation temperature?

For me, a variable thermostat is a much more important feature than a timer. This capability allows you to fine-tune your recipe and determine the incubation temperature you prefer. You can always set a kitchen timer if you need a reminder. And because each batch of yogurt is different and you can never be sure how long it will take to set, a timer isn't particularly useful. You need to check regularly to determine when the yogurt has set.

can read about the two-temperature, "high-low" method it recommends for yogurt making, which has worked well for me. The proofer accommodates eight quart jars, and it folds flat for storage.

If you are not using a yogurt-making appliance, you will need to create a warm environment for incubating your yogurt. The target temperature range is not easy to maintain for several hours. Some people successfully incubate yogurt in their gas oven with only the warmth of the pilot light. (Alas, many newer ovens do not have pilot lights.) If you want to try this, preheat the oven to the lowest setting first, and then turn it off. Test the temperature after half an hour and then hourly to see if the oven remains within the target range for at least 5 hours. If it does, it should work as an incubator.

Some people use an insulated container, such as a picnic cooler, partially filled with warm water as an incubator. Others wrap yogurt jars in an electric blanket or set them on a heating pad or in a jury-rigged Styrofoam container with a low-wattage light bulb. You can also keep the incubating yogurt in a consistently warm spot in your house, such as near a radiator or sunny window. A food dehydrator with removable shelves can work as an incubator if the temperature can be set low enough. Some people use a countertop slow cooker, heating the milk slowly in the device and then unplugging it to cool the milk to the culturing temperature. Wrapping the pot with towels after culturing helps maintain temperature.

When I don't use an electric appliance, I incubate my yogurt the way home cooks have for centuries: wrapped in blankets. (I use small throw blankets.) First, I wrap my warm, just-filled quart jars in kitchen dish towels so they won't soil the blankets. Then I snuggle the jars into a blanket nest—a blanket underneath and another on top and, if the house is cold, another blanket around them for good measure. Then I ignore the heap for 4 to 5 hours before unwrapping it to check for set. If the milk has not set yet, I check it every half hour or so thereafter.

Whichever incubation method you choose, avoid jostling the yogurt as it incubates. It prefers to be undisturbed.

Homemade Yogurt

MAKES 1 QUART

1 quart milk of any type

2 tablespoons instant nonfat dry milk
(optional but recommended)

2 tablespoons plain yogurt with
live active cultures, at room temperature

This recipe can be doubled.
You will need an instant-read
thermometer, available at
any housewares store.

WHY HEAT THE MILK?

Even if you are using a freshly opened container of pasteurized milk, you should heat it to at least 185°F before culturing. Pasteurization kills pathogens but it doesn't sterilize the milk. By heating the milk to 185°F (or higher, as I describe), you eliminate competitors to the desirable bacteria in your culture. Just as important, you denature more milk proteins so that they coagulate as a single mass rather than as clumpy curds. Yogurt made from heated milk is more stable and less likely to "whey off," or release whey.

GETTING READY

Assemble all necessary equipment. You don't want to be rummaging around for jar lids when your milk is ready to culture. Make sure that all equipment is scrupulously clean, with no soap residue that could damage the culture.

HEATING THE MILK

Pour the milk into a 2- to 3-quart stainless steel saucepan. Whisk in the instant nonfat dry milk, if using. Set the pan over medium-low heat. Whisking often to prevent the milk from scorching, heat until the milk registers 195°F on an instant-read thermometer. Adjust the heat as needed to keep the milk at or near 195°F and cook, whisking often, for 10 minutes. (Note: The extended cooking at 195°F produces a thicker yogurt. See "Troubleshooting" sidebar, page 20, for an explanation. For thinner yogurt, heat the milk only to 180°F or 185°F and remove from the heat when it reaches that temperature.)

COOLING THE MILK

Cover the saucepan and let the milk cool to between 110°F and 115°F, about 1¼ hours. (It may take longer if you are making a larger volume.) You can dramatically accelerate the cooling by placing the saucepan in a large bowl or sink full of ice water and stirring constantly. The milk temperature will plummet to the culturing range in less than 5 minutes, so monitor often. If it drops too low (below 110°F), return the saucepan to the stove top and rewarm the milk over low heat just until it reaches 110°F to 115°F.

PREPARING THE JARS

While the milk cools to the proper culturing temperature, prepare the jars. Choose a 1-quart jar or smaller jars with a total capacity of 1 quart; or use the jars that come with your yogurt maker. Wash well, and then fill the jars with hot water and let stand until you need them. Replace the hot water if it cools so the jars will be warm when you fill them. Drain just before filling. Alternatively, heat the jars with hot water, and then drain and place in a preheated electric yogurt maker to keep warm until you are ready to fill them.

Note that you don't have to use jars. You can incubate yogurt in a glass or earthenware bowl, or in any nonreactive (nonaluminum) container. You can even incubate it in the saucepan you heated the milk in. However, once the yogurt has set, you need to chill it to stop the fermentation and firm the curd, so make sure your incubation container will fit in

TROUBLESHOOTING

If your yogurt isn't thick enough:

- Add instant nonfat dry milk powder to raise the protein content of the milk. More protein will produce a thicker and more stable set. Use 2 tablespoons instant nonfat dry milk per 1 quart of fluid milk.

- Try using higher-fat milk, such as whole milk. Adding half-and-half or cream to whole milk will make a particularly rich yogurt. Even just 20 percent half-and-half (1 cup half-and-half to 4 cups milk) will make a noticeable difference.

- Try heating the milk to 195°F—higher than many recipes suggest—and holding it at that temperature for 10 minutes. The extended heating denatures lactoglobulin, a whey protein, so it can be captured in the yogurt and contribute to thickness.

- Incubate longer. Give the yogurt another hour or two at incubation temperature to allow the culture to work some more.

- Drain the yogurt (see page 22). Removing whey produces a thicker yogurt and extends refrigerated shelf life.

- Try another culture—either another brand of yogurt or another source of dried culture. If you are using homemade yogurt for your inoculant, the bacteria may be sluggish, especially if the yogurt is more than one week old.

If your yogurt is slimy or "ropy":

- When the incubation temperature is too low—below 104°F—the bacteria tend to form more polysaccharides, which give yogurt that unpleasant slippery texture. Try to raise the incubation temperature slightly: a range of 108°F to 112°F will make the starter culture happy.

the fridge. You don't want to transfer just-set yogurt to other containers, or you will damage the fragile curd.

CULTURING THE MILK

If you are using yogurt as your culture, put the yogurt in a small, clean bowl and whisk in about 1 cup of the cooled milk. Pour this mixture back into the saucepan and whisk gently but well. You want to incorporate the culture well without creating a lot of foam. Immediately transfer the milk to the prepared jar or jars and cover.

If you are using a purchased dried culture, follow the manufacturer's directions for inoculation.

INCUBATING THE YOGURT

Incubate according to your chosen method (see page 16) until the yogurt thickens and firms. Avoid moving or otherwise agitating the yogurt while it ferments. Check for set after 4 hours and at least once per hour after that.

IS IT DONE YET?

Yogurt can take anywhere from 4 to 12 hours to gel, or even longer, depending on the incubation temperature and the strength of the culture. The longer it takes, the more tart your yogurt will be, as the culture continues to produce lactic acid. I prefer mellow yogurt, so I try to stop the incubation as soon as the yogurt has firmed.

To check for set, tilt the jar slightly. If the yogurt looks like baked custard and doesn't flow, it has set sufficiently. If it is jiggly and you want it firmer, let it incubate longer. Incubating longer should make it a little more tart and firm, but you can overincubate it. If whey has collected on the surface, the yogurt probably fermented a little too long or too fast and is starting to separate. Either pour off the surface whey or, after chilling the yogurt, stir it back in. Don't try to stir the whey in before chilling the yogurt, as the curd will be too fragile.

Don't be concerned if each batch of yogurt you make is a little different. Unlike commercial producers with their controlled processes, your home yogurt "factory" is subject to variability: in the milk and culture used, the way you heated and cooled the milk, the length of the fermentation, and the fermentation temperature. Experiment, make notes, and over time you will find the combination of culture, time, and temperature that produces yogurt with the texture and flavor you like.

Making
Drained Yogurt

I often drain yogurt, especially homemade yogurt, even if only for an hour. Draining dramatically improves the texture, making any yogurt thicker, creamier, and more mellow by removing whey. Draining also extends the yogurt's life by removing water and lactose. Reducing the yogurt's lactose deprives bacteria of their food source. And if you are lactose-sensitive, you should find drained yogurt more digestible.

To drain homemade yogurt, chill it thoroughly first until it is firm. You can drain it as soon as it is cold. Store-bought yogurt has already been chilled, so you can drain it immediately after opening.

Line a large sieve or colander with a triple thickness of dampened cheesecloth or—my preference—with Plyban, a reusable cheesecloth made from a food-grade resin (see Resources, page 135). Plyban's weave is tighter than cheesecloth, so you don't need multiple layers, although with very thin yogurt I might use a double thickness.

Set the sieve or colander over a bowl to collect the whey. Gently pour the yogurt into the lined sieve or colander. Cover with a plate or cloth—you're just protecting the yogurt, not pressing it—and refrigerate.

Drain the yogurt until it has the consistency you like. After an hour, it will be noticeably thicker, and I usually stop at that point. Scrape the drained yogurt into a clean container, cover, and refrigerate.

Wash the cheesecloth or Plyban well in hot, soapy water; rinse well and air-dry. You can usually get two or three uses out of cheesecloth before it frays. Plyban is much longer-lasting and easier to clean.

If you drain the yogurt more than you intended, no problem. Simply whisk some of the whey back in until you have a texture you like.

To keep the whey, pour it into a glass jar and refrigerate. It has many potential uses (see page 23).

Making Greek Yogurt

Greek yogurt is essentially drained yogurt, although manufacturers use more sophisticated methods than home yogurt makers do (see page 5). To make Greek yogurt, follow the procedure for "Making Drained Yogurt" but instead of stopping at an hour, keep going. When the yogurt has lost about half of its volume—when a quart has been reduced to 2 cups—it will have the dense, palate-coating texture of Greek yogurt. Depending on the yogurt you started with, this might take 3 to 4 hours.

Making Yogurt Cheese

Follow the procedure for "Making Drained Yogurt." After 2 hours of draining, stir in ½ teaspoon kosher or sea salt for every quart of yogurt that you started with. Return to the refrigerator and continue draining until the yogurt is as thick as cream cheese, about 24 hours total. From a quart of milk, you should yield 1½ to 1¾ cups of yogurt cheese.

Using Whey

Whey is the cloudy, yellowish liquid that leaches out of yogurt over time. In a partially consumed container of yogurt, you can usually see whey pooling in the low spots. In homemade yogurt, it may collect at the top of a full container, especially if you incubated the yogurt a little too long. You can drain it off or stir it in once the yogurt is fully chilled. If you drain yogurt to thicken it (see page 22), what drains out is whey. It is largely water, but it includes some lactose, protein, vitamins, and minerals, so whey has some nutritional value.

In frugal households, whey isn't discarded. Many people enjoy its tart, lemony taste, especially when the whey is chilled. You can drink it as you might consume buttermilk, or add it to smoothies or cold soups. You can experiment with using it as a buttermilk supplement or replacement in baked goods, like pancakes and biscuits. Some people use whey to inoculate vegetable fermentations such as sauerkraut, or in place of some of the water in bread dough. Because of the lactose, it enhances browning. Amaryll Schwertner, a noted San Francisco chef, tells me that she uses whey in meat marinades; the acid functions as a tenderizer.

Whey also has a reputation for nourishing skin and hair. Some beauty experts advocate conditioning your hair with a whey rinse or applying it to the face with a cotton puff, like toner.

Yogurt
for
Breakfast

If you start your day with a bowl of yogurt, you share a morning ritual with millions of people around the world. Maybe you prefer your breakfast yogurt with sliced bananas and brown sugar, while an office worker in Istanbul has crisp cucumbers and olive oil with his. Either way, yogurt makes a wholesome foundation for the day, especially when paired with fruit, grains, and nuts.

You don't need a recipe to tell you how to spoon yogurt over peaches, but perhaps you could use a nudge to try some new combinations. Many of us operate on autopilot in the morning, our brains too groggy for decisions, our routines fixed. But it takes so little effort to make breakfast a little different today than it was yesterday, so that you sit down to the meal with anticipation and consider it an important way to power up for the day.

Yogurt with Fresh Fruit

Pair yogurt with fresh fruit, of course, but try to choose fruit in season. You'll eat better and save money. Plain yogurt complements almost every type of fruit imaginable, but Southern Hemisphere raspberries in January have too many miles on them and too little flavor. Why not replace them with some orange segments or sliced kiwifruit?

To guide you to fruit in season, here's a rough month-by-month harvest calendar based on a typical year in California, which supplies a lot of the nation's fresh fruit. Crops in your region may appear a little earlier or later. Of course, many fruits straddle seasons, and nature always has the last word.

JANUARY: grapefruits, mandarin oranges, navel oranges, other citrus

FEBRUARY: grapefruits, mandarin oranges, navel oranges, other citrus

MARCH: blood oranges

APRIL: pineapples

MAY: mangoes, rhubarb, strawberries

JUNE: apricots, cherries, figs

JULY: blackberries, blueberries, nectarines, peaches, raspberries

AUGUST: apples, grapes, melons, plums and pluots

SEPTEMBER: apples, dates, figs, grapes, melons, pears

OCTOBER: apples, grapes, pears, pomegranates, quinces

NOVEMBER: cranberries, persimmons

DECEMBER: kiwifruit, kumquats, persimmons, tangerines

YEAR-ROUND: bananas, papayas

Yogurt with Eggs

However you like your eggs in the morning, yogurt can dress them up:

- Stir dollops of yogurt cheese (page 23) into scrambled eggs just before you serve them.
- Top fried or poached eggs with whisked room-temperature yogurt and a red-pepper drizzle (page 66).
- Fill an omelet with nuggets of yogurt cheese (page 23) and wilted spinach.
- Make egg salad with drained or Greek yogurt and chopped dill, chives, or chervil; serve with whole-grain toast.

Yogurt with Nuts & Seeds

Nuts and seeds add another dimension to a bowl of yogurt and fruit, a pleasing crunch that boosts satisfaction. Consider almonds, cashews, pecans, walnuts, hazelnuts, pistachios, peanuts, pumpkin seeds, and sesame seeds. Toasting nuts improves their flavor. Preheat an oven to 325°F, spread the nuts or seeds on a rimmed baking sheet, and bake until fragrant and lightly colored. Nuts and seeds contain oils that eventually go rancid. Keep untoasted nuts and seeds in the refrigerator or freezer to extend their life. After toasting, store them in an airtight container and use within a month.

Yogurt with Other Natural Sweeteners

If you like sweetened yogurt, stock your pantry with a variety of sweeteners to shake up your routine. In place of granulated sugar, try an aromatic local honey, brown sugar, maple syrup, agave nectar, jaggery (date-palm sugar), date syrup, or pomegranate molasses.

Yogurt with Granola

Granola loves yogurt and vice versa, but the calorie tally can soar. Some store-bought granolas—especially the bulk-bin blends—are hardly more wholesome than candy. Pay attention to the ingredients list and calorie count, and look for a mix that highlights the grains. A layered parfait of yogurt, fresh or cooked fruit, and granola (page 111) makes a portable breakfast that you can change up daily with seasonal fruit.

Yogurt with Fruit Preserves

Use a dollop of store-bought or homemade fruit preserves to sweeten yogurt. Middle Eastern markets often have intriguing options like rose-petal jam, quince preserves, and fig jam. In Greek markets, look for jarred "spoon sweets" made with sour cherries, apricots, walnuts, or watermelon. Spoon sweets can be intense—closer to candied fruit than preserves—but a small serving can elevate a bowl of yogurt. For a brunch, set out a big bowl of plain yogurt with an array of exotic preserves and locally made jams.

Yogurt with Dried Fruit

In winter and early spring, when fresh-fruit choices are slim, I often pair yogurt with dried fruit: peaches, nectarines, figs, prunes, pears, apricots, apples, cherries, and grapes (raisins) dried with no added sugar. You can poach the fruit in light sugar syrup, but often I simply plump the fruit in water for a few hours to soften it without cooking. Dates are so moist that they need no softening. Pit them, then slice or chop and serve them with yogurt, toasted walnuts, and honey.

To plump dried fruit: Soften the dried fruit in cool water for several hours, or use warm water to speed the process. I use just enough water to cover so I don't dilute the soaking liquid. When the fruit is soft, taste the liquid. If it is sweet enough for you, transfer the fruit and liquid to a lidded container; cover and refrigerate. If it isn't sweet enough, drain the liquid into a saucepan and add sugar to taste, a strip of lemon or orange peel, and maybe a smacked cardamom pod or two, or a bit of cinnamon bark. Simmer until the sugar dissolves and the syrup thickens slightly. Cool completely, and then pour back over the fruit. Transfer to a lidded container, cover, and refrigerate.

Plumped dried fruit will keep for 2 to 3 weeks in the refrigerator, so make a generous batch. You can mix plumped fruits, but mix them after soaking as some take longer to soften than others.

MIXED MARRIAGES: A DOZEN FRESH BREAKFAST IDEAS

Try your yogurt with . . .

- pitted fresh cherries, honey, and toasted pecans.
- red and black grapes, grape jelly, and roasted peanuts.
- bananas, toasted sliced almonds, and orange marmalade.
- raspberries and raspberry jam.
- dates, honey, and toasted sesame seeds.
- pineapple and brown sugar.
- baked apples and cinnamon sugar.
- grapefruit and avocado.
- Hachiya persimmon and maple sugar.
- fresh apricots and toasted pistachios.
- sliced peaches and granola.
- kiwifruit, mandarin oranges, and toasted coconut.

Appetizers & Salads

Cool, creamy yogurt salads are beloved in countries where yogurt reigns. India has its raita, a refreshing counterpoint to grilled meats and curries; Greece, its tzatziki. In Iran, the typical cucumber-yogurt salad includes raisins, walnuts, and mint (page 39), an enchanting combination. Around the Eastern Mediterranean, yogurt enriches smoky eggplant puree (page 40). In this chapter, you will encounter some of these traditional uses for yogurt as well as more contemporary ideas, such as a juicy farro salad with yogurt underneath (page 48).

Roasted Tomato Bruschetta *with* Yogurt Cheese

SERVES 6

6 plum (Roma) tomatoes (about 1 pound), halved lengthwise

2 tablespoons extra-virgin olive oil

1½ teaspoons dried oregano

2 cloves garlic, finely minced

Kosher or sea salt

12 baguette slices, cut on the diagonal about ½ inch thick

¾ cup yogurt cheese (page 23)

Fresh basil leaves, for garnish

Slow-roasting concentrates the flavor of plum tomatoes and caramelizes their natural sugars. If you stop the roasting while the softened tomato halves still hold their shape, they will make a juicy topping perfectly sized to fit baguette toasts. A schmear of tangy yogurt cheese under the tomato balances the sweetness.

Preheat an oven to 300°F. Put the tomatoes cut side up in a shallow baking dish just large enough to hold them in a single layer. Drizzle with the olive oil. Season with the oregano, crumbling the dried herb between your fingers to release its fragrance. Dot the tomatoes with the minced garlic and season with salt. Bake until the tomatoes are very soft and beginning to caramelize but still hold their shape, 2 to 3 hours, depending on their size and ripeness. Using a pastry brush, baste the tomatoes with any pan juices—the tomatoes may not release much—every 45 minutes or so. Let cool slightly. The tomatoes are best warm, not hot.

Preheat a broiler or toaster oven. Place the baguette slices on a baking sheet and toast on both sides until golden brown.

Spread one side of each toast with 1 tablespoon yogurt cheese. Top with a warm roasted tomato half. (You can halve the tomatoes lengthwise first so they cover more of the toast surface.) Garnish with the basil leaves and serve immediately.

Yogurt Cheese *with* Feta, Pumpkin Seeds & Za'atar

SERVES 4

2 dozen Niçoise olives or other
unpitted black olives

1½ to 2 tablespoons extra-virgin olive oil,
plus more for drizzling on the olives

1 cup yogurt cheese (page 23)

1 small clove garlic, grated or finely minced
(see note, page 88)

Kosher or sea salt

⅓ cup crumbled feta cheese

1 teaspoon za'atar
(see Resources, page 135)

1 tablespoon store-bought toasted
and salted pumpkin seeds

Medium-hot coarsely ground red pepper
such as Aleppo or Maraş pepper
(see note, page 82), or hot paprika

Persian or English hothouse cucumbers,
cut into thin spears

Radishes, preferably several varieties,
any ragged leaves trimmed

Sprigs of mint or dill

Skillet Flatbread (page 70),
store-bought flatbread, or pita

This communal Middle Eastern *meze* (appetizer) is more about arranging ingredients than about cooking them. A bed of creamy yogurt cheese topped with feta, olive oil, pumpkin seeds, and *za'atar*—a Middle Eastern spice blend—makes an exotic dip for vegetables. I've suggested a few possibilities, but feel free to embellish with green onions, raw fennel, or cooked beets. Tear off some flatbread, scoop up some cheese, and wrap around a sprig of mint and a cucumber spear. I first encountered this beautiful *meze* at a Persian restaurant near San Francisco—since closed, alas—and I've been enamored of it ever since.

Preheat an oven to 325°F. Put the olives in a shallow baking dish, drizzle lightly with olive oil, and toss to coat. Bake until warm throughout, about 5 minutes. Keep warm while you prepare the rest of the dish.

Stir together the yogurt cheese, garlic, and salt to taste. Using a rubber spatula, spread on a plate in a thin pool, making sure to create some indentations where olive oil can puddle. Sprinkle the feta on top. Drizzle with the 1½ to 2 tablespoons olive oil and sprinkle with the *za'atar*. Scatter pumpkin seeds over all and sprinkle with the red pepper. Surround with the warm olives, cucumbers, radishes, and mint sprigs. Serve warm flatbread alongside.

Cucumber Salad with Yogurt, Golden Raisins, Walnuts & Mint

SERVES 4 TO 6

¼ cup golden raisins

2 cups plain yogurt

1 cup plain drained yogurt (page 22)
or Greek yogurt (not nonfat)

1 to 2 cloves garlic, grated or finely minced
(see note, page 88)

1 tablespoon chopped fresh dill,
plus more for garnish

1 teaspoon finely minced fresh mint

Kosher or sea salt

2 cups ¼-inch-diced Persian or English
hothouse cucumber (no need to peel)

⅓ cup coarsely chopped toasted walnuts
(see page 29)

Cucumber and yogurt salad is part of the repertoire in every yogurt-eating country, but for me the star recipe is this one. I love the burst of sweetness from the raisins, the crunch of walnuts, the coolness of mint. The salad complements grilled lamb, or you could serve it as part of a *meze* assortment with flatbread. I like to use the crisp, thin-skinned, nearly seedless Persian cucumbers—also called Mediterranean cucumbers—that are about six inches long. Najmieh Batmanglij, the author of several Persian cookbooks that I admire, garnishes her version of this salad with dried rose petals. If you have unsprayed rose petals in the garden, they would make a pretty garnish, too. Break into smaller pieces and scatter on top.

I like this salad to have a thicker, creamier texture than I can get from plain yogurt alone, so I add a little drained or Greek yogurt for extra body.

Put the raisins in a small bowl, add barely enough water to cover, and let plump for at least 1 hour. Drain.

In a large bowl, whisk together the yogurts, garlic, 1 tablespoon dill, mint, and salt to taste. Add the raisins, cucumbers, and walnuts. Stir well, and then taste and adjust the seasoning. Serve immediately, garnished with more chopped dill, or cover and refrigerate for up to 1 hour. If you want to hold the salad longer, leave the walnuts out initially and add them just before serving to preserve their crunch.

Smoky Eggplant Salad with Pita Crisps

SERVES 4

1 large Italian eggplant or small globe eggplant (about 1 pound)

2 tablespoons extra-virgin olive oil, plus more for garnish

½ yellow onion, minced

2 cloves garlic, minced

Kosher or sea salt and freshly ground black pepper

½ cup plain yogurt

¼ to ½ teaspoon toasted and ground cumin seeds (see note, page 45)

Chopped cilantro, for garnish

Pita Crisps (recipe follows)

A deep, smoky taste from slow grilling and the caramelized flavor of fried onions make this creamy spread irresistible. Even if you don't have a grill, you can infuse the eggplant with a smoky note by cooking it slowly over a stove-top gas flame. I'm indebted to Paula Wolfert for the idea of using a roasting rack to keep the eggplant propped above the stove-top flame.

Pierce the eggplant in several places with a small knife to allow steam to escape. Prepare a moderate charcoal fire under one half of your grill rack, leaving the other half devoid of coals so you can grill the eggplant over indirect heat. Alternatively, preheat a gas grill to medium, leaving one burner unlit for indirect grilling.

Set the eggplant near the coals or gas flame, but not directly over. Cover the grill and cook the eggplant, turning occasionally with tongs, until it is charred all over and thoroughly cooked, about 30 minutes. The dense flesh at the stem end is usually the last to soften, so be sure to check doneness there. The area should feel soft when probed.

Alternatively, set a stainless steel V-rack (the type used for roasting chicken) over a burner on a gas stove set to medium-low. Place the eggplant in the V-rack as far from the flame as possible and cook slowly, turning with tongs, until the eggplant is charred all over and thoroughly cooked, 30 to 40 minutes. Move it around on the rack as needed to ensure that the dense stem end cooks through.

Let the eggplant cool, and then halve lengthwise and scrape out the flesh with a spoon. Discard the skin and any blackened bits of skin that may cling to the flesh. Chop the flesh coarsely, conserving any juices.

Heat the olive oil in a 10-inch skillet over medium heat. When the oil is hot, add the onion and sauté, stirring almost constantly, until it softens and turns golden brown, about 5 minutes. Reduce the heat if necessary to keep the onion from burning. Add the garlic and sauté 1 minute to release its fragrance. Add the eggplant and any juices and season with salt and pepper. Cook briskly, stirring vigorously, until the excess moisture evaporates and the eggplant begins to stick to the skillet, about 2 minutes. Do not let it scorch. Remove from the heat and let cool for about 5 minutes.

Stir in the yogurt and ¼ teaspoon of the ground cumin. Season with salt, taste, and add more cumin if desired.

To serve, spread the eggplant salad on a shallow plate. Drizzle with additional olive oil. Garnish with cilantro. Serve warm or at room temperature, with the Pita Crisps.

Pita Crisps

MAKES 16 TO 24 CRISPS

2 pita rounds
2 tablespoons extra-virgin olive oil
Kosher or sea salt

Preheat an oven to 375°F. Using your hands, carefully tear each pita in half along the "equator" to yield half-moons, each with a pocket. Gently open the half-moons and separate the pockets at the rounded edge so that you have eight half-moon pieces. Arrange them on a baking sheet— it's okay if they overlap slightly—and brush them on both sides with the olive oil. Rearrange them on the baking sheet rough side up and season lightly with salt. Bake until they are richly browned throughout and crisp, 8 to 12 minutes, transferring them as they are done to a cooling rack. When cool, break each piece into 2 or 3 smaller chips.

Cherry Tomato Raita

SERVES 4

1 cup plain drained yogurt (page 22)
or Greek yogurt (not nonfat)

½ teaspoon sugar

¼ cup finely minced red onion

2 to 3 tablespoons coarsely
chopped cilantro

1 clove garlic, grated or finely minced
(see note, page 88)

½ serrano chile, finely minced
(remove seeds for less heat, if desired)

½ pound cherry tomatoes,
preferably mixed colors

1 tablespoon plus 2 teaspoons vegetable oil

½ teaspoon brown mustard seeds

½ teaspoon whole cumin seeds

Kosher or sea salt

When your garden or farmers' market yields sun-sweetened cherry tomatoes, remember this raita—an Indian-style yogurt salad with warm toasted spices. I could happily have it for lunch with nothing but flatbread or warm pita, but like other raitas, it complements grilled foods. Add it to the menu whenever you're serving grilled lamb, chicken, burgers, or fish. For a meatless meal, serve it with saffron rice and charcoal-grilled summer squash.

In a bowl, whisk the yogurt with the sugar. Stir in the red onion, cilantro, garlic, and chile.

Halve the cherry tomatoes, or quarter them if large. In a 10-inch skillet, warm 1 tablespoon of the vegetable oil over high heat. Add the tomatoes and sauté briskly until the tomatoes soften and render some juice, 1 to 2 minutes, depending on ripeness; don't allow them to collapse into a sauce. Scrape the tomatoes and their juices into the yogurt.

In a small skillet or butter warmer, warm the remaining 2 teaspoons vegetable oil over medium heat. Have the skillet lid handy. When the oil is hot, add the mustard seeds and cumin seeds. Protecting your face with the skillet lid, cook until the mustard seeds pop and the cumin darkens and becomes highly fragrant, 1 minute or less. Pour the hot oil and seasonings over the yogurt and stir in.

Let the raita rest at room temperature for 30 minutes to allow the flavors to develop. You can cover and refrigerate the raita for a couple of hours, but remove from the refrigerator about 30 minutes before serving to take the chill off. Just before serving, season to taste with salt. The raita should be loose and spoonable, neither soupy nor stiff. Thin with a little water if necessary.

Roasted Cauliflower Raita

SERVES 4

3 packed cups bite-size cauliflower florets (about 10 ounces)

2 tablespoons peanut or vegetable oil

Kosher or sea salt and freshly ground black pepper

1½ cups plain yogurt

1 clove garlic, grated or finely minced (see note, page 88)

1 teaspoon brown mustard seeds

½ teaspoon whole cumin seeds

¼ large yellow onion, thinly sliced

1 serrano chile, halved, seeded, and thinly sliced lengthwise

12 fresh curry leaves, or more if small

A raita, or yogurt salad, is a mealtime staple in many Indian homes, especially on vegetarian tables. The yogurt contributes protein and a cooling complement to spicier dishes, even when the raita itself packs some warmth. I've enjoyed cucumber raita countless times, and eaten many raitas made with cooked vegetables like seared tomatoes and roasted eggplant. I had never had a cauliflower raita, but the idea appealed to me, knowing how compatible the vegetable is with Indian seasonings. Roasting the vegetable intensifies its flavor and slightly chars the edges. You can serve this raita with grilled lamb kebabs or chops or just make a simple dinner of raita and rice pilaf.

Look for fresh curry leaves in Indian markets. They have a nutty, toasty fragrance that is mesmerizing. Alas, there is no adequate substitute. The raita will be tasty without them, but curry leaves make it sing.

Preheat an oven to 400°F. Put the cauliflower florets in a bowl with 1 tablespoon of the oil and salt and pepper to taste. Toss with your hands until the florets are evenly coated with oil and seasonings. Arrange them in a single layer on a parchment-lined baking sheet and bake until they become tender and slightly charred on the edges, about 30 minutes. Cool slightly.

In a large bowl, whisk the yogurt with the garlic. Season to taste with salt.

Have the mustard seeds, cumin seeds, onion, chile, and curry leaves measured and ready near the stove. In a small skillet, heat the remaining 1 tablespoon oil over medium-high heat. Keep the skillet lid handy. When the oil is hot, add the mustard seeds and cumin seeds. Protecting your face with the skillet lid, cook until the mustard seeds pop and the cumin darkens and becomes highly fragrant, 1 minute or less. Add the onion, chile, and curry leaves. Reduce the heat to keep the onion from scorching. Sauté, stirring almost constantly, until the onion is golden brown, about 3 minutes. Scrape the contents of the skillet into the yogurt, and then fold in the cauliflower. Taste for salt. You can serve the raita immediatelyor let it rest at room temperature for an hour or two. Refrigerate for longer keeping, but bring to room temperature before serving.

Grated Carrot & Yogurt Salad with Cumin

SERVES 4

1 pound carrots

2 tablespoons extra-virgin olive oil

Kosher or sea salt

1 cup plain yogurt

1 large clove garlic, grated or finely minced
(see note, page 88)

Scant ½ teaspoon toasted and ground
cumin seeds (see note)

Freshly squeezed lemon juice

Chopped fresh parsley or cilantro,
for garnish

TOASTING AND GRINDING CUMIN SEEDS

Ground cumin is much more fragrant if you make it from whole seeds that you toast and grind only as needed. Put the seeds in a small dry skillet and cook over moderate heat, swirling the pan often, until the cumin darkens and becomes fragrant, 2 to 3 minutes. Let cool, and then grind into a fine powder in a mortar or spice grinder.

Ayla Algar's recipe for cooked carrots in yogurt in *Classical Turkish Cooking* inspired this adaptation. I have made Algar's recipe many times, often with some modest alterations. She seasons her salad with chopped dill. I like it with toasted cumin and a big squeeze of lemon. You could add some plumped golden raisins or fold in chopped pistachios.

Serve this salad as part of an assortment of *mezedes*, with feta, olives, and flatbread. Or use as a side dish with grilled lamb or sausage. I prefer it at room temperature or even slightly warm. You can chill it, but it will thicken; loosen it up with a little cool water (or whey from a container of yogurt) and adjust the seasoning before serving.

Peel the carrots and grate them coarsely. (I use the coarse holes on a box grater.) You should have about 4 cups.

In a heavy 12-inch skillet, heat the olive oil over high heat. Add the carrots, season with salt, and cook, stirring almost constantly with a wooden spoon, until the carrots soften and wilt slightly, 3 to 4 minutes. They should no longer be crunchy. Transfer the carrots to a large bowl.

In another bowl, whisk together the yogurt, garlic, cumin, and salt to taste.

Add the yogurt to the warm carrots and stir to blend. Taste and add more salt if needed; brighten the flavor with lemon juice to taste. Scatter parsley or cilantro over the top and serve at room temperature.

Grated Beet & Yogurt Salad *with* Beet Greens

SERVES 6

8 beets of any color,
with greens attached

1 tablespoon white wine vinegar,
plus more as needed

1½ cups plain drained yogurt (page 22)
or Greek yogurt (not nonfat)

1 to 2 teaspoons finely minced
fresh tarragon

1 large clove garlic, grated or finely minced
(see note, page 88)

Kosher or sea salt

½ cup coarsely chopped toasted walnuts
(see page 29)

TARRAGON DRESSING

3 tablespoons extra-virgin olive oil

1 tablespoon freshly squeezed lemon juice

½ teaspoon Thai or Vietnamese fish sauce

½ teaspoon minced fresh tarragon

1 small clove garlic, finely minced
(see note, page 88)

Kosher or sea salt

When you buy beets with the greens attached, you get two vegetables for the price of one. I wince when I hear a farmers' market shopper ask the grower to remove the tops, and I don't hesitate to pipe up and say, "I'll take those." Only in America, where produce is cheap, would people think the leaves aren't worth eating. They are rich in nutrients and a good indicator of freshness. If the greens are perky, the beets were just pulled.

For this dish, I roast and thickly grate the beets and then fold them into garlicky yogurt. Alongside, I serve the boiled greens, dressed simply with olive oil, lemon juice, and tarragon or dill. If the stems are thick and meaty, I prepare them, too—first cutting them into shorter lengths, and then boiling or steaming them and adding them to the greens.

The beets in yogurt can be made several hours ahead and refrigerated, though they taste best when they aren't refrigerator-cold. I prefer the greens warm, so I cook them shortly before serving and don't rinse them with cold water.

Preheat an oven to 375°F. Remove the beet greens, leaving about ½ inch of stem attached to the beets to avoid cutting into them. Separate the beet leaves from the stems. (If the stems are thick, meaty, and firm, you can cook and dress them as well; see recipe introduction. Otherwise, discard them.) Wash and drain the leaves.

Put the beets in a baking dish large enough to hold them in a single layer. Add ½ inch of water. Cover tightly and bake until the beets are tender when pierced with a small knife or skewer, about 1 hour. Cool slightly, and then peel. (They are easier to peel while still warm.) Grate the beets on the coarse holes of a box grater. You should have about 3 cups. Put the beets in a bowl and add the vinegar. Toss well.

In a large bowl, whisk together the yogurt, 1 teaspoon of the tarragon, the garlic, and salt to taste. Fold in the grated beets and walnuts. Taste and adjust the seasoning, adding more tarragon or vinegar if desired.

To make the dressing: In a small bowl, whisk together the olive oil, lemon juice, fish sauce, tarragon, garlic, and salt to taste.

Bring a large pot of salted water to a boil over high heat. Add the beet greens and simmer until tender, about 2 minutes. Drain in a sieve or colander. When just cool enough to handle, squeeze dry and chop coarsely.

Put the warm beet greens in a bowl and add enough of the dressing to coat them lightly. You may not need it all. (Reserve any leftover dressing for salads.) Toss the greens with your hands until they are evenly dressed. Taste and add more salt or lemon if needed. Arrange the beet greens on one end of a platter and the grated beet salad on the other end, or serve the greens and beet salad in separate bowls.

Radish Tzatziki

SERVES 6

½ pound red radishes (about 16), grated on the coarse holes of a box grater

1½ cups plain drained yogurt (page 22) or Greek yogurt (not nonfat)

2 packed tablespoons chopped fresh dill

1 clove garlic, grated or finely minced (see note, page 88)

Pinch of sugar

Kosher or sea salt

White wine vinegar (optional)

For a departure from the traditional cucumber tzatziki that every Greek restaurant serves, try this pretty version with grated radish. I love the ruby flecks from the radish skin, but pink-fleshed watermelon radishes would also work. (Be sure to peel watermelon radishes thickly before grating; they have a hard exterior.) Serve as part of a *meze*, or appetizer, spread, with black olives, stuffed grape leaves, feta, and flatbread, or as a condiment for grilled meats.

Wrap the grated radishes in a clean dish towel and squeeze well to remove excess moisture. Set the radishes aside. You should have about 2 cups.

In a large bowl, whisk together the yogurt, dill, and garlic. Season to taste with sugar and salt. Fold in the radishes. Taste and add more salt as well as a splash of vinegar, if desired.

Chopped Summer Vegetable Salad *with* Farro, Yogurt & Za'atar

SERVES 4

½ cup semi-pearled farro

GARLIC VINAIGRETTE

3 tablespoons extra-virgin olive oil

1 tablespoon white wine vinegar,
plus more if needed

1 teaspoon Thai or Vietnamese fish sauce

1 clove garlic, finely minced
(see note, page 88)

Kosher or sea salt

1 cup plain yogurt

1 large clove garlic, grated or finely minced
(see note, page 88)

1 tablespoon za'atar
(see recipe introduction, page 36)

½ pound cucumbers, preferably Persian,
Japanese, or English hothouse variety

½ cup thinly sliced green onions,
white and pale green parts only

½ cup loosely packed whole cilantro leaves
(no stems)

2 to 3 tablespoons coarsely chopped
fresh mint

1 large handful small arugula, watercress,
or purslane leaves (no thick stems)

½ pound ripe but firm tomatoes,
cut into ⅓-inch dice

½ large ripe but firm avocado,
cut into ⅓-inch dice

Inspired by the juicy bulgur salads of the Mediterranean and Middle East, this chopped summer vegetable salad features farro. Known as emmer in English, farro (the Italian word) is a type of wheat with a particularly nutty taste and pleasing chewiness. The cooked grains soak up the dressing without becoming sticky or soft, and they give this salad enough heft to serve for lunch. With farro's growing popularity, markets now carry several types. Look for lightly pearled farro (*semi-perlato* on Italian brands), which you can recognize by the slightly abraded appearance of the exterior, the bran layer. Whole, unpearled farro takes much longer to cook and doesn't absorb the dressing as well.

Bring 3 cups of salted water to a boil in a small saucepan over high heat. Add the farro and reduce the heat to medium; skim off any surface foam. Cover partially, adjust the heat to maintain a gentle simmer, and cook until the farro is al dente—fully cooked but still firm to the tooth—about 30 minutes. Drain well in a sieve, and then transfer to a large bowl.

To make the dressing: In a small bowl, whisk together the olive oil, vinegar, fish sauce, garlic, and salt to taste.

Spoon about 1½ tablespoons dressing over the farro, enough to coat it lightly, and toss well with a fork. Taste and add more salt or a splash of vinegar if needed.

In a small bowl, whisk together the yogurt, garlic, and salt to taste. Make a bed of yogurt sauce on a large platter, using it all. Sprinkle the *za'atar* over the yogurt.

If the cucumbers have a thick or waxed skin, peel them; if not, then leave unpeeled. Halve the cucumbers lengthwise. If they have large seeds, scrape out the seeds with a small spoon. If the seeds are small, no need to remove. Cut the cucumber into ⅓-inch dice and add to the farro along with the green onions, cilantro, and mint. Add more dressing and toss gently to mix. Add the arugula, tomatoes, and avocado. Drizzle with the remainder of the dressing and toss gently to avoid breaking up the tomatoes and avocado. Taste for salt and vinegar.

Using your hands, mound the farro salad on top of the yogurt, leaving a visible border of yogurt. Serve immediately.

Soups

Whether drizzled on a spicy split-pea soup (page 53) or blended with golden beets and garlic (page 59), yogurt invigorates soups hot and cold. In chilly weather, a chicken soup with toasted pasta, chickpeas, and yogurt (page 55) warms up the kitchen; when it's too hot to cook, a chilled avocado soup with salsa (page 61) has enormous appeal. In this chapter, yogurt proves its worth as both soup enrichment and appetizing garnish.

Spicy Yellow Split Pea Soup
with
Tomato, Cumin & Yogurt

SERVES 6

2 cups yellow split peas, rinsed

2 bay leaves

1 teaspoon ground turmeric

1 small dried red chile, broken in half

1 quart chicken or vegetable broth
(low-sodium if canned)

1 quart cold water

¼ cup ghee (see note, page 87)
or vegetable oil

1 teaspoon whole cumin seeds

1 yellow onion, halved
and thinly sliced

4 cloves garlic, thinly sliced, plus 1 clove
garlic, grated or finely minced
(see note, page 88)

2 large plum (Roma) tomatoes, halved
lengthwise, seeded, and thinly
sliced lengthwise

Kosher or sea salt

¾ cup plain whole-milk yogurt

Chopped cilantro, for garnish

With its toasted Indian seasonings, this soup fills the kitchen with lusty fragrance. It reheats well, so you can cart it to a potluck or take some to a sick friend. For a perfect winter dinner, accompany with a crunchy green salad—maybe escarole with sliced fennel and radishes—and open a favorite beer. You can make the soup with green split peas, but I think yellow ones have a finer flavor, and the saffron-yellow soup looks especially appetizing with yogurt drizzled on top.

Put the split peas, bay leaves, turmeric, and chile in a large saucepan. Add the chicken broth and cold water. Bring to a simmer over medium heat, and then cover and adjust the heat to maintain a gentle simmer. Cook until the split peas are soft and breaking down, 30 minutes or more, depending on their age. The mixture will be brothy at this point, but if it seems too thin, uncover and continue simmering until it thickens to a soup consistency that you like.

Heat the ghee in a large skillet over medium-high heat. Add the cumin seeds and cook, swirling the skillet, until the seeds darken and become fragrant, less than 1 minute; do not let them burn. Add the onion and sliced garlic. Reduce the heat to medium and cook, stirring almost constantly, until the onion browns, about 5 minutes. Reduce the heat to medium-low if needed to keep the onion from burning, but it should fry, not sweat. Add the tomatoes, raise the heat to high, and cook, stirring constantly, until the tomatoes soften slightly, 1 to 2 minutes. Stir the contents of the skillet into the lentils. Use a few tablespoons of water to deglaze the skillet and add that liquid to the lentils, too. Season the soup with salt. Remove the bay leaves and chile. Keep the soup hot.

In a small bowl, whisk the yogurt with the grated garlic and salt to taste. If necessary, whisk in a little cool water so the yogurt is thin enough to drizzle.

Divide the soup among 6 bowls. Drizzle the yogurt on top, dividing it evenly. Garnish with the chopped cilantro. Serve immediately.

Yogurt, Leek & Barley Soup *with* Red-Pepper Butter

SERVES 4 TO 6

1 quart chicken broth

½ pound skinless, boneless chicken thighs

⅓ cup pearled barley

1 cup thinly sliced leeks, white and pale green parts only

1½ cups plain yogurt (not nonfat)

1½ tablespoons all-purpose flour

1 large egg yolk

2 packed tablespoons chopped fresh dill, plus more for garnish

Kosher or sea salt and freshly ground black pepper

2 teaspoons unsalted butter

½ teaspoon medium-hot coarsely ground red pepper such as Aleppo or Maraş pepper (see note, page 82), or hot paprika

Yogurt-thickened soups such as this one are staple fare around the Eastern Mediterranean, sometimes with rice, chickpeas, or bulgur in place of barley; or with lamb instead of chicken. I use thighs because the meat has more flavor than breast meat and stays moist, but you can substitute chicken breast, if you prefer.

In a pot, combine the chicken broth and chicken thighs. Bring the broth to a simmer over medium heat, skimming any foam. Cover and adjust the heat to maintain a gentle simmer. Cook for 5 minutes, and then remove from the heat and allow the thighs to steep in the hot liquid until just cooked through, 5 to 10 minutes longer, depending on size. Remove the thighs with tongs and, when cool enough to handle, shred the meat into bite-size pieces.

Add the barley to the broth and return to a simmer. Cover partially, adjust the heat to maintain a gentle simmer, and cook for 20 minutes. Add the leeks and continue simmering gently, partially covered, until the barley is tender, 10 to 15 minutes longer.

In a large bowl, whisk together the yogurt, flour, egg yolk, and dill. Whisk in about half of the soup to warm the yogurt, and then pour the mixture into the soup pot, whisking constantly. Add the shredded chicken. Cook over medium-low heat, stirring constantly with a wooden spoon, until the soup just begins to simmer. Season to taste with salt and black pepper. Divide among warmed bowls.

In a small pan or butter warmer, melt the butter over medium heat. When it sizzles and foams, add the pepper and swirl for a few seconds to bring out the pepper fragrance. Drizzle some of the sizzling butter over the surface of each soup, dividing it evenly. Garnish with a little more chopped dill and serve immediately.

Chicken Soup *with* Toasted Pasta, Chickpeas & Yogurt

SERVES 4

1½ tablespoons unsalted butter

6 ounces spaghetti, broken into approximately 1-inch lengths (about 2 cups)

1 quart chicken or vegetable broth, simmering

1½ cups cooked chickpeas, rinsed well if canned

2 cups plain yogurt (not nonfat)

2 large egg yolks

2 tablespoons chopped Italian parsley

1 tablespoon plus 1 teaspoon all-purpose flour

Scant 1 teaspoon dried spearmint or 2 tablespoons chopped fresh mint

Kosher or sea salt and freshly ground black pepper

Medium-hot coarsely ground red pepper such as Aleppo or Maraş pepper (see note, page 82), or hot paprika

Toasting the pasta before simmering it in broth imparts a nutty, brown-butter flavor to this creamy soup. I use spaghetti or spaghettini, broken into short lengths so the pasta is easy to eat with a spoon. Dried spearmint is actually preferable to fresh mint here; the dried herb, with its sweet aroma, gives this soup a proper Turkish taste.

In a large soup pot, melt the butter over medium-low heat. Add the broken spaghetti and toast, stirring constantly, until the pasta turns a rich golden-brown and has the nutty aroma of brown butter, 3 to 5 minutes. Watch closely; once the pasta begins to color, it darkens quickly. Do not let the butter burn.

Slowly add the hot broth—it will hiss and bubble up. Stir in the chickpeas and bring to a simmer. Cover, adjust the heat to maintain a gentle simmer, and cook until the pasta is almost tender, about 10 minutes.

In a large bowl, whisk together the yogurt, egg yolks, parsley, and flour. If using spearmint, rub it between your fingers to crush it finely. Whisk the mint into the yogurt mixture. Gradually whisk in about 2 cups of the hot broth, tilting the pot as needed to collect the broth. Pour the warmed yogurt mixture into the pot, stirring constantly. Cook, uncovered and stirring with a wooden spoon, until the soup just comes to a simmer. Season with salt and pepper.

Divide the soup among warmed bowls. Top each portion with a dash of red pepper. Serve immediately.

Shredded Beet & Cabbage Soup *with* Yogurt

SERVES 8

1 pound red beets (weight without greens, about 4 medium or 3 large)

½ pound carrots

1 tablespoon extra-virgin olive oil

3 thick slices bacon, halved lengthwise and diced

1 yellow onion, minced

2 or 3 cloves garlic, minced

¾ pound Savoy cabbage, cored and shredded

1 bay leaf

1½ quarts rich chicken, beef, or vegetable broth

Kosher or sea salt and freshly ground black pepper

1 cup plain drained yogurt (page 22) or Greek yogurt (not nonfat), at room temperature, whisked

Chopped fresh dill, for garnish

This beet-red soup may resemble borscht at a glance, but its flavor is fresher and more delicate. Even so, it's a supper for a chilly night, served perhaps with hot cornbread or rye toast and whipped butter. For the best results, prepare a rich homemade broth or choose the best available store-bought brand; the soup needs a strong foundation because it has so little meat. Use whole-milk yogurt for the topping so it doesn't break when you stir it in.

Preheat an oven to 375°F. Remove the beet greens if attached, leaving 1 inch of stem to avoid cutting into the beets. Put the beets in a baking dish with ½ inch of water. Cover and bake until the beets are tender when pierced, 1 to 1¼ hours. When cool enough to handle, peel the beets and grate them on the coarse holes of a box grater.

If the carrots are large, halve or quarter them lengthwise first, and then slice crosswise ¼ inch thick.

Heat the olive oil in a large, heavy pot over medium heat. Add the bacon and cook, stirring, for about 5 minutes to render some of the fat. Add the onion and garlic and cook, stirring often, until the onion is soft and beginning to color, about 10 minutes. Add the carrots, cabbage, beets, and bay leaf and stir to blend. Add the broth and bring to a simmer. Cover, adjust the heat to maintain a gentle simmer, and cook until the carrots and cabbage are just tender, about 20 minutes. Season to taste with salt and pepper. Remove the bay leaf.

Divide the soup among warmed bowls. Top each portion with 2 tablespoons of yogurt and a generous pinch of dill. Serve immediately.

Creamy Tomato & Bulgur Soup *with* Yogurt

SERVES 4

3 large ripe plum (Roma) tomatoes

1 quart chicken or vegetable broth

2 tablespoons extra-virgin olive oil

½ large yellow onion, minced

1 teaspoon medium-hot coarsely ground red pepper such as Aleppo or Maraş pepper (see note, page 82), or hot paprika

Kosher or sea salt

1 long green Anaheim chile, halved lengthwise, seeds removed, and thinly sliced crosswise

1 cup extra-coarse (no. 4) or coarse (no. 3) bulgur (see Resources, page 135)

½ cup plain whole-milk yogurt

1 large clove garlic, grated or finely minced (see note, page 88)

¼ cup minced fresh cilantro or dill, or a combination

Aglaia Kremezi's charming cookbook, *The Foods of the Greek Islands*, introduced me to *hondros*, a risotto-like bulgur pilaf with tomato, green chile, and feta. I make it often, and it occurred to me that similar ingredients would make a terrific soup, with yogurt replacing the feta and the addition of more broth. The yogurt, stirred in at the end, contributes a silky texture and subtle tang.

This is a thick and rustic soup, simple yet nourishing, like the best rural Greek food. The longer it stands, the thicker it gets because the bulgur continues to swell. It doesn't reheat well—the bulgur overcooks—so plan to serve it shortly after it is made. I prefer the texture of extra-coarse bulgur here (see Resources, page 135). Manufacturers identify it on the package as the no. 4 size. Coarse bulgur (no. 3 size) will work, but finer bulgur will not give good results.

Halve the tomatoes lengthwise and grate them on the coarse holes of a box grater until only the skin remains in your hand. You should have about ¾ cup of tomato pulp. Discard the skin.

Bring the broth to a simmer in a small saucepan; cover partially and reduce the heat to low.

Heat the olive oil in a heavy pot over medium-low heat. Add the onion and red pepper and sauté until the onion is soft and sweet, 5 to 10 minutes. Add the tomato pulp and a pinch of salt, raise the heat to medium-high, and sauté for about 2 minutes to soften the tomato and concentrate its flavor. Reduce the heat to medium, add the Anaheim chile and bulgur, and stir until the bulgur is hot throughout, about 1 minute.

Add the hot broth and bring to a simmer. Taste for salt. Cover and reduce the heat to low. Cook for 15 minutes, and then remove from the heat and let stand 10 minutes longer.

In a small bowl, whisk together the yogurt, garlic, herbs, and salt to taste. Whisk in about 1 cup of the hot soup, and then stir the warmed yogurt mixture into the soup. Taste again for salt and serve.

Chilled Golden Beet & Yogurt Soup

SERVES 4 TO 6

1 pound golden beets (weight without greens, about 3 medium to large)

3 cups plain whole-milk yogurt

1 large clove garlic, sliced

Kosher or sea salt

Champagne vinegar or white wine vinegar

Thinly sliced chives, for garnish

I don't know an easier soup, or a more appealing one on a balmy evening. You can add fresh herbs to the blender—chives, tarragon, and dill are all complementary—but I prefer to put the herbs on top to preserve the soup's cornmeal color.

Preheat an oven to 375°F. Remove the beet greens, if attached, leaving ½ inch of stem to avoid cutting into the beet. Put the beets in a baking dish with ½ inch of boiling water. Cover and bake until the beets are tender when pierced, 50 minutes or longer, depending on size. When cool enough to handle, peel the beets and cut into large chunks. (They are easier to peel while still warm.) Let cool to room temperature.

Put the yogurt in a blender along with the beets and garlic. Blend until completely smooth. If the soup is a little too thick for your taste, add a couple of ice cubes and blend again. Transfer to a bowl and stir in salt to taste. Chill thoroughly. Just before serving, taste again and adjust the seasoning, adding more salt and a splash of vinegar to balance the beets' sweetness. You will probably need only 1 teaspoon or so.

Divide among bowls or mugs. Top each portion with sliced chives.

Chilled Avocado & Yogurt Soup with Tomato Salsa

SERVES 6

2 large ripe but firm avocados

1½ cups buttermilk

1½ cups plain yogurt

2 heaping tablespoons chopped cilantro

1 large clove garlic, thinly sliced

½ serrano or jalapeño chile, seeds removed
for less heat if desired, or more to taste

½ teaspoon toasted and ground cumin seeds
(see note, page 45)

1 tablespoon freshly squeezed lime juice

Kosher or sea salt

SALSA

1 large plum (Roma) tomato, halved
lengthwise, seeded, and cut into ¼-inch dice

¼ cup finely minced white onion

2 heaping tablespoons chopped cilantro

½ serrano or jalapeño chile, seeds removed
for less heat if desired, finely minced

1 small clove garlic, finely minced

Kosher or sea salt

Freshly squeezed lime juice

All the flavors of guacamole meet up in this creamy soup, with yogurt adding body and refreshment. Serve with Pita Crisps (page 41) or tortilla chips. For lunch, add a salad of frisée, jicama, and oranges. For dinner, serve in small portions and follow with grilled ribs, grilled salmon, or just about anything grilled.

Halve and pit the avocados. Set aside half an avocado for the salsa. Put the remaining avocado flesh in a blender with the buttermilk, yogurt, cilantro, garlic, chile, and cumin. Blend until smooth. Taste and add more chile if desired, and then blend again. Transfer to a bowl and stir in enough cold water to thin the soup to a pleasing consistency, about ½ cup. Stir in the lime juice, or more to taste, and season with salt. Chill thoroughly.

Just before serving, prepare the salsa: In a bowl, stir together the tomato, onion, cilantro, chile, and garlic. Cut the reserved avocado half into ¼-inch dice and fold it in gently, and then season to taste with salt and lime juice and stir again gently to avoid mashing the avocado.

If the soup has thickened in the refrigerator, whisk in ice water to thin it to the desired consistency. Taste for seasoning. Divide among 6 bowls. Top each serving with a spoonful of salsa and serve.

Mostly Meat

Yogurt plays a variety of valuable roles in meat cookery.
Used as a marinade, it tenderizes meat and enhances browning; the
recipe for harissa-roasted chicken (page 65) will persuade you of that.
A garlicky yogurt sauce complements roasted or grilled lamb, a pairing
that underlies the timeless popularity of Greek souvlaki (page 68).
Yogurt can add body to pan juices, as it does for lamb meatballs
(page 66) and braised lamb with artichokes (page 74). Although
yogurt rarely appears with seafood, a creamy tahini-yogurt sauce
makes an irresistible companion for grilled swordfish (page 79).

Harissa-Roasted Chicken *with* Sweet Peppers

SERVES 6

½ cup plain drained yogurt (page 22) or Greek-style yogurt (not nonfat)

½ cup coarse harissa paste (see note)

1 tablespoon freshly squeezed lemon juice

Kosher or sea salt and freshly ground black pepper

6 bone-in, skin-on chicken thighs, trimmed of excess skin

2 large red bell peppers, halved, seeded, and thinly sliced

2 large gold or yellow bell peppers, halved, seeded, and thinly sliced

1 large red onion, halved and thinly sliced

HARISSA PASTE

Harissa paste comes in tubes, like toothpaste, but my favorite brand is a jarred one, Les Moulins Mahjoub Organic Traditional Harissa Spread. The recipe includes hot red pepper, sun-dried tomato, olive oil, caraway, and garlic. If you can't find harissa paste, purchase dried harissa powder from a spice shop and add enough extra-virgin olive oil to make a paste. Ask the merchant about the ingredients in the powder. If the blend doesn't contain ground caraway, add a good pinch. Look for Les Moulins Mahjoub harissa in specialty foods stores that sell Mediterranean products. It is also available from several online sources, including Zabar's, iGourmet, Market Hall Foods, and Bklyn Larder.

The yogurt marinade makes this chicken especially tender and juicy, while the harissa stains it brick-red and adds tongue-tingling spice. Depending on how fiery your harissa is, you may want to increase or reduce the amount you use. Taste and adjust the marinade before adding the raw chicken.

I've adapted this recipe from one given to me by Ed Blonz, a clinical nutritionist and syndicated columnist, who makes it when his book club comes for dinner. Ed roasts the chicken on a bed of chickpeas and onions. I like it with sweet peppers underneath. The vegetables absorb the spicy drippings from the chicken and need no further seasoning.

If your menu includes several other dishes, figure one chicken thigh per person. Otherwise, you may want to allow two thighs per person. The roasted chicken benefits from a brief rest to allow the juices to settle.

In a large bowl, whisk together the yogurt, harissa, lemon juice, 1 teaspoon salt, and several grinds of black pepper. Add the chicken and use a rubber spatula to coat the chicken all over with the marinade. Cover and refrigerate for 4 to 8 hours. Remove from the refrigerator 30 minutes before baking.

Position a rack in the upper third of an oven and preheat the oven to 425°F.

Toss the sliced peppers and onions together. Season with salt and make a bed of the vegetables in the bottom of a roasting pan large enough to hold the chicken in a single layer. Using a rubber spatula, redistribute the marinade so that it evenly covers both sides of the chicken, and then place the chicken on top of the vegetables. Bake until the chicken is well browned on top and the vegetables are tender, about 40 minutes. Remove from the oven and let rest for 10 minutes.

Transfer the chicken to a serving platter. Using tongs, toss the vegetables to coat them evenly with the drippings from the chicken, and then place them on the platter with the chicken. Serve immediately.

Lamb Meatballs in Warm Yogurt Sauce *with* Sizzling Red-Pepper Butter

SERVES 4 TO 6

LAMB MEATBALLS

1 pound ground lamb

1 large egg, lightly beaten

½ cup fine fresh bread crumbs

½ cup finely minced yellow onion

1 teaspoon dried oregano

1 teaspoon kosher or sea salt

½ teaspoon toasted and ground cumin
seeds (see note, page 45)

Freshly ground black pepper

1 tablespoon extra-virgin olive oil
1 cup chicken broth

2 cups plain whole-milk yogurt

1 large egg, lightly beaten

2 cloves garlic, grated or finely minced
(see note, page 88)

2 tablespoons chopped fresh dill,
plus more for garnish

1 tablespoon minced fresh mint

2 teaspoons unsalted butter

½ teaspoon medium-hot coarsely ground
red pepper such as Aleppo or Maraş
pepper (see note, page 82), or hot paprika

½ teaspoon toasted and ground cumin
seeds (see note, page 45)

A gem of a recipe from the Eastern Mediterranean kitchen, these succulent meatballs bathe in a sauce that will have you scraping the bowl. I have seen similar recipes for whole lamb shanks or chunks of shoulder, but meatballs cook more quickly. They are browned first, and then simmered in broth, but the magic happens just before serving, when yogurt and a beaten egg are whisked in to thicken the juices. Sizzling red-pepper butter provides a final flourish. Serve with bulgur or rice pilaf, or with egg noodles.

To make the meatballs: Combine all the ingredients and mix well with your hands. Shape into 24 balls, dipping your hands in cold water as needed to keep the mixture from sticking.

Heat a 12-inch skillet over medium heat. Add the olive oil and swirl to coat. When the oil is hot, add the meatballs; they should fit in a single layer. Fry gently, turning the meatballs with two soup spoons so they brown on all sides, about 5 minutes. Using a slotted spoon, transfer the meatballs to a plate. Pour off and discard any fat in the skillet.

Return the skillet to medium-high heat and add the broth. Stir with a wooden spoon to scrape up any browned bits on the bottom of the skillet and simmer until they dissolve. Return the meatballs to the skillet, cover, and reduce the heat to maintain a gentle simmer. Cook for 10 minutes, and then transfer the meatballs to a plate using a slotted spoon.

In a large bowl, whisk together the yogurt, egg, garlic, dill, and mint. Slowly whisk in about ½ cup of the hot broth to warm the yogurt, and then pour the yogurt mixture into the skillet. Cook over medium-low heat, stirring with a wooden spoon, until the sauce visibly thickens and just begins to simmer. Add salt and pepper to taste. Return the meatballs to the skillet and turn to coat them with the sauce. Cover and simmer gently until hot.

Divide the meatballs and sauce among 4 to 6 warmed bowls. Put the butter in a small saucepan or butter warmer and set over medium heat. When the butter melts, add the red pepper and cumin and swirl the pan until the butter foams and sizzles and the pepper's aroma rises. Drizzle each portion with some of the red-pepper butter. Garnish with chopped dill.

Lamb Souvlaki *with* Skillet Flatbread

SERVES 4

1 tablespoon extra-virgin olive oil

1 tablespoon freshly squeezed lemon juice

¾ teaspoon dried oregano, crushed fine

¾ teaspoon garlic powder

½ teaspoon kosher or sea salt

Freshly ground black pepper

¾ pound leg of lamb, neatly trimmed
of all fat, cut into ¾-inch cubes

YOGURT SAUCE

1½ cups plain yogurt

1 large clove garlic, grated or finely minced
(see note, page 88)

Kosher or sea salt

Skillet Flatbread (recipe follows) or
store-bought flatbread

2 tablespoons extra-virgin olive oil

1 large clove garlic, finely minced

½ pound cherry tomatoes, halved

¾ teaspoon medium-hot coarsely ground
red pepper such as Aleppo or Maraş
pepper (see note, page 82), or hot paprika

Kosher or sea salt

¼ cup coarsely chopped cilantro,
for garnish

Grilled meat on a skewer: it's the most primitive kind of cooking, but if you tend to the details, the succulent outcome may make you dream of starting your own street-food stand. In this version of souvlaki, the beloved Greek kebab, an oregano- and garlic-laced marinade seasons the lamb. Halved cherry tomatoes warmed in olive oil make a juicy topping that complements the yogurt sauce. (A mix of red and gold tomato varieties would be eye-catching.) Using a Near Eastern red pepper, such as Maraş or Aleppo—or, even better, the smoked Urfa pepper from Turkey—gives the result the most authentic taste. And you will not regret taking the time to make your own flatbread.

I've suggested serving flatbread wedges on the side, for scooping up the mingled juices, but you can also put a whole flatbread on each plate and spoon yogurt sauce, grilled lamb, and cherry tomatoes on top. You can substitute pork, beef, or chicken for the lamb—or offer guests an assortment.

In a bowl large enough to accommodate the lamb, whisk together the olive oil, lemon juice, oregano, garlic powder, salt, and several grinds of black pepper. Add the lamb and toss to coat well. Cover the bowl and refrigerate for about 4 hours. If you would like to marinate the lamb longer (up to 1 day ahead), omit the lemon juice, adding it a couple of hours before cooking.

Prepare a hot charcoal fire or preheat a gas grill to high. Thread the lamb onto 4 metal or bamboo skewers. (If using bamboo, presoak the skewers in water for 30 minutes to prevent burning.)

To make the yogurt sauce: In a bowl, whisk together the yogurt, garlic, and salt to taste. Cover and let stand at room temperature for 1 hour.

Unless you have just made the Skillet Flatbread, wrap flatbreads in aluminum foil and reheat in a moderate oven.

In a small skillet, warm the olive oil over medium heat. Sauté the garlic until it is fragrant and starting to color, about 1 minute. Add the tomatoes, red pepper, and salt to taste.

continued

Sauté, stirring, until the tomatoes soften and are hot throughout, but don't allow them to collapse into a sauce. Keep warm.

Grill the lamb directly over the coals or gas flame until done to your taste, about 5 minutes for medium-rare.

Divide the yogurt sauce among 4 dinner plates. Remove the lamb from the skewers and place the meat on top of the yogurt. Top with the warm tomatoes and juices, dividing them evenly. Garnish with cilantro. Cut the warm flatbreads into triangles, put a few on each plate, and pass the rest separately. Serve immediately.

Skillet Flatbread

MAKES 6 FLATBREADS

SPONGE

1 cup warm water (105°F to 110°F)

1½ teaspoons active dry yeast

1 cup unbleached all-purpose flour

FLATBREAD DOUGH

2½ cups unbleached all-purpose flour, plus more for dusting

½ cup whole wheat flour

2½ teaspoons kosher or sea salt

⅓ cup plain whole-milk yogurt

¼ cup extra-virgin olive oil, plus more for frying

½ cup water

I learned this method of pan-frying flatbread from chef Erik Cosselmon of Kokkari, a Greek restaurant in San Francisco.

To make the sponge: Put the warm water in a bowl and sprinkle the yeast over it. Let the yeast soften for about 2 minutes, and then whisk to dissolve. Let stand until bubbly, about 5 minutes. Using a wooden spoon, stir in the flour and mix until smooth. Cover the bowl and let the sponge ferment in a cool place for at least 4 hours and up to 1 day.

To make the dough: In a bowl, whisk together the all-purpose flour, whole wheat flour, and salt. Put the sponge in the bowl of a stand mixer fitted with the paddle attachment. Add the yogurt, ¼ cup olive oil, and water. Blend on low speed. Add the flour mixture gradually, beating on low speed. When blended, raise the speed to medium and knead for 5 minutes. The dough will be moist. Scrape down the sides of the bowl and the paddle, cover the bowl with plastic wrap, and let the dough rise at room temperature for 1½ hours.

Turn the dough out onto a floured work surface; the dough will be sticky. Divide into 6 equal pieces (a scale is helpful here), dusting each piece lightly with flour to keep it from sticking to the board or your hands. Shape each piece into a ball and set on a large sheet of parchment paper, leaving enough room between the balls for them to double in size. Dust the tops lightly with flour and cover with a clean dish towel. Let rise for 1½ hours.

To fry the flatbreads, heat a 10-inch skillet over medium-low heat. Add 2 teaspoons olive oil and swirl to coat the bottom of the skillet. Working with 1 ball of dough at a time, shape into an evenly thick 8-inch round just large enough to cover the bottom of the skillet. You can use a rolling pin, but I find it easier to stretch the dough by hand, draping it over the back of my fists and gradually enlarging the round, as a pizza maker would.

When the oil shimmers, place the round in the hot skillet. Cook until golden brown, about 3 minutes, and then flip with a metal spatula. Cook the second side until golden brown, about 3 minutes longer. Adjust the heat so the flatbread does not darken too much before it cooks through; it needs at least 6 minutes of cooking time. Transfer to a rack and repeat with the remaining rounds, adding fresh oil each time. Let cool for 15 minutes before cutting into wedges.

Orzo *with* Spicy Lamb, Chickpeas & Yogurt

SERVES 4

2 tablespoons extra-virgin olive oil, plus more if needed

1 pound boneless lamb leg or shoulder (weighed after trimming), trimmed of visible fat and gristle, and cut into 1/3-inch dice

Kosher or sea salt

1 large yellow onion, chopped

2 cloves garlic, minced

1 tablespoon tomato paste

1 jalapeño chile, quartered lengthwise, seeds removed for less heat if desired

1 teaspoon sweet paprika

2½ cups homemade or low-sodium canned chicken broth

1 bay leaf

½ cinnamon stick

¼ teaspoon saffron threads

1 cup cooked chickpeas, rinsed well if canned

1 cup dried orzo pasta

½ cup plain drained yogurt (page 22) or Greek yogurt, whisked well

Chopped Italian parsley, for garnish

San Francisco's esteemed Greek restaurant Kokkari serves its delectable lamb shanks with orzo (rice-shaped pasta) moistened with the lamb braising juices. That taste memory led me to devise a similar dish made with a lamb sauce, as a whole shank can often be too much for one person. The Greek seasonings—cinnamon, saffron, paprika, and green chile—will perfume your kitchen. A cool dollop of yogurt on top softens the spice.

Lamb stew cut from the leg throws little fat and works well in this sauce. If your butcher has some lamb bones, add them to the sauce and fish them out before serving. They will enhance the body. You can also use lamb shoulder—my preference—but it is fattier and requires more trimming. If you do use shoulder, you may want to chill the sauce long enough for the fat to rise so you can skim it off before adding the chickpeas. Either way, trim the lamb fastidiously and dice it small. It takes some time, but the hand-diced lamb is much more satisfying than ground lamb or large chunks.

Most supermarkets sell orzo, but brands vary in length. I prefer the long orzo that resembles wild rice in size over orzo that looks more like short-grain rice.

Heat 2 tablespoons olive oil in a large, heavy Dutch oven or high-sided skillet over medium-high heat. Add the lamb, season with salt, and brown on all sides. If the lamb releases juices, cook until they evaporate. Transfer the lamb to a plate with a slotted spoon and add the onion to the pot. Add another 1 tablespoon olive oil, if needed. Reduce the heat to medium-low and sauté the onion until softened, about 10 minutes. Add the garlic and sauté for 1 minute to release its fragrance. Add the tomato paste, chile, paprika, broth, bay leaf, cinnamon stick, and saffron. Bring to a simmer, stirring with a wooden spoon to dissolve the tomato paste and any browned residue on the bottom and sides of the pan.

Return the lamb to the skillet. Bring to a simmer and taste the liquid for salt. Cover and adjust the heat to maintain a bare simmer. Cook until the lamb is tender, about 45 minutes for lamb leg, 1¼ hours for lamb shoulder. Stir in the chickpeas. Simmer gently, covered, for about 5 minutes to infuse the chickpeas with flavor. Adjust the seasoning. Remove the bay leaf and cinnamon stick. Keep the lamb sauce warm while you cook the pasta.

Bring a large pot of salted water to a boil over high heat. Add the orzo and cook until almost al dente. (It will continue cooking in the sauce.) Drain the pasta and return it to the warm pot. Tilt the pot containing the lamb sauce and scoop off enough of the flavorful liquid to moisten the pasta. Add the liquid to the orzo and cook over medium heat, stirring, until the pasta is hot and well moistened with sauce, about 1 minute. Taste for salt.

Divide the orzo among 4 warmed bowls, and then top each portion with the lamb sauce, dividing it equally. Spoon 2 tablespoons of yogurt on top of each portion, and then garnish with parsley. Serve immediately.

Braised Lamb Shoulder *with* Artichokes, Peas & Yogurt

SERVES 4

2 pounds bone-in lamb shoulder chops

Kosher or sea salt and freshly ground black pepper

1 tablespoon extra-virgin olive oil

2 large yellow onions, halved and thinly sliced

2 large cloves garlic, minced

½ cup chicken broth mixed with ½ cup water

1 sprig fresh mint

1 dozen fresh baby artichokes (1½ to 2 ounces each) or 1 dozen frozen artichoke hearts, thawed and quartered

1 lemon

1 cup fresh English peas or frozen petite peas

1 cup Greek yogurt (not nonfat), at room temperature

2 packed tablespoons chopped fresh dill

The underappreciated lamb shoulder chops are far more succulent than rib or loin chops, and their bones contribute body and flavor to this braise. Thick yogurt, added at the last moment, enriches the meaty juices. Serve with steamed bulgur or rice, potatoes, or pasta. Fresh egg noodles or dried orzo or orecchiette are also good choices.

Cut the chops lengthwise into 2 pieces, maneuvering around the bones. Trim external fat and any visible chunks of fat that you can easily reach. Season the pieces on both sides with salt and pepper.

Choose a heavy 12- to 14-inch skillet or wide-bottomed pot large enough to accommodate all the meat in a single layer with the vegetables tucked in the crevices. Heat the skillet over medium-high heat, and then add the oil and swirl to coat the bottom. Add the lamb and brown on both sides, 3 to 4 minutes per side. Using tongs, transfer the lamb to a plate and reduce the heat to medium-low. Add the onions and cook, stirring often with a wooden spoon, until soft and browned, 10 to 15 minutes. The moist onions should help dissolve some of the meaty residue on the skillet bottom. Add the garlic and cook until fragrant, about 1 minute.

Return the lamb to the skillet with any juices collected on the plate. Add the broth/water mixture and the mint sprig. Bring to a simmer, cover, and adjust the heat to maintain a gentle simmer. Cook for 1 hour.

If you are using fresh artichokes, trim them while the lamb cooks: Fill a medium bowl with water and add the juice of the lemon. Peel back the outer artichoke leaves until they break off at the base. Keep removing leaves until you reach the pale green heart. Cut across the top of the heart to remove the pointed leaf tips. If the stem is still attached, cut it down to ½ inch, and then trim the stem and base to remove any dark green or brown parts. Quarter each heart and immediately place in the lemon water to prevent browning.

When the lamb has cooked for 1 hour, drain the artichokes and add them to the skillet. Baste them with pan juices and push them down into the liquid. Cover and cook at a gentle simmer until both the lamb and the artichokes are tender, 20 to 25 minutes.

If you are using fresh peas, bring a small pot of salted water to a boil over high heat. Add the peas and boil until just tender, 3 to 5 minutes. Drain. Add them to the skillet when the artichokes and lamb are tender, and stir to coat with the sauce. They only need to heat through.

If you are using frozen artichokes or peas, braise the lamb until fork-tender, 1¼ to 1½ hours, before stirring in the frozen vegetables; cover the pan again and simmer gently until they are hot.

In a bowl, whisk together the yogurt, dill, and a generous pinch of salt. Slowly whisk in about 1 cup of the braising juices. Remove the skillet from the heat and gently stir in the yogurt mixture with a wooden spoon. Taste and adjust the seasoning. Serve immediately in bowls.

Grilled Hanger Steak
with Grilled
Red Onion Raita

SERVES 4

1⅓ to 1½ pounds hanger steak

1 teaspoon kosher or sea salt

1 teaspoon mixed peppercorns
(white, black, green, pink), crushed in
a mortar or with a pepper grinder

RED ONION RAITA

1 large red onion (10 to 12 ounces)

Vegetable oil

Kosher or sea salt and freshly
ground black pepper

1 cup plain whole-milk yogurt

1 clove garlic, grated or finely minced
(see note, page 88)

1 tablespoon finely minced cilantro or
1½ teaspoons finely minced fresh mint

¼ teaspoon toasted and ground cumin
seeds (see note, page 45)

½ teaspoon mustard seeds

Grilled red onion adds sweet and smoky notes to this raita (yogurt salad). Be patient and cook the onion slowly so it softens fully and develops that campfire aroma. Folded into yogurt with toasted cumin and mustard seeds, the chopped red onion makes an unusual raita to serve with grilled beef, lamb burgers, or chicken thighs. I think hanger steak is one of the most underrated cuts on the steer. It has a tough membrane running through it that you have to grapple with—directions follow—but the rich, beefy flavor will reward you.

Hanger steak has a tough membrane running down the center. You can leave this membrane in place, trimming it away as you eat the steak, or you can remove it before grilling. The latter is my preference, as the meat is easier for guests to eat with no pesky membrane to cut around. To remove the membrane, use a boning knife or other sharp knife to slice carefully on either side of it and lift it out cleanly, with little or no meat attached. You will be left with 2 disconnected strips of hanger steak. Rearrange them side by side and tie in several places with butcher's twine to re-create a single steak.

Combine the salt and crushed pepper. Season the meat all over with the mixture. Set a flat rack on a tray and set the meat on the rack so air circulates underneath. Refrigerate, uncovered, for at least 4 hours and up to 1 day. Remove from the refrigerator 1 hour before grilling.

Prepare a moderate charcoal fire in the center of your grill, leaving the outer rim devoid of coals so you can grill the red onions over indirect heat. Alternatively, preheat a gas grill to medium, leaving one burner unlit for indirect grilling.

To make the raita: Peel the onion and slice neatly into ½-inch-thick rounds. Carefully thread a thin bamboo skewer through each slice to hold the rings together. Brush the slices with oil on each side, and season with salt and pepper on each side. Grill over indirect heat—not directly over the coals or gas flame—turning once, until the onions are soft and slightly charred, about 25 minutes. Do not rush them or they will blacken before they are fully cooked. Transfer to a cutting board and pull out the skewers. If the outer ring of the onion

continued

slices is dry and papery, discard it. Chop the remainder of the onion coarsely.

In a bowl, whisk together the yogurt, garlic, cilantro or mint, and cumin. In a small skillet or butter warmer, warm 2 teaspoons vegetable oil over medium heat. Have the skillet lid handy. When the oil is hot, add the mustard seeds. Protecting your face with the lid, cook until the mustard seeds pop and become fragrant, 1 minute or less. Pour the hot oil and mustard seeds over the yogurt and stir in. Fold in the grilled onion. Season the raita with salt.

Grill the hanger steak directly over the coals or gas flame, turning once, until the meat is done to your taste, about 10 minutes for rare. (Hanger steak is best if not cooked beyond medium-rare.) Let rest 5 minutes. Remove the string (if you tied the meat) and slice thinly against the grain. Serve immediately with the red onion raita.

Grilled Swordfish *with* Yogurt Tahini Sauce & Sumac

SERVES 6

6 swordfish steaks, each about 6 ounces and no more than ½ inch thick

Extra-virgin olive oil

Kosher or sea salt and freshly ground black pepper

½ cup plain whole-milk yogurt

¼ cup creamy tahini (if oil has separated, stir well before measuring)

1 or 2 cloves garlic, grated or finely minced (see note, page 88)

¼ cup freshly squeezed lemon juice, or more to taste

3 tablespoons finely minced cilantro

3 tablespoons finely minced Italian parsley

About 1½ teaspoons ground sumac

6 lemon wedges

I rarely want more on grilled fish than olive oil and lemon, but this tangy yogurt-tahini sauce is an exception. It mingles deliciously with the swordfish juices and complements the smoky notes from the grill. You can use the sauce with grilled tuna, lamb, zucchini, and eggplant as well.

Most fishmongers slice swordfish too thickly, in my opinion. Contrary to what you might expect, a thin swordfish steak, grilled quickly, will be more tender than a thick one, and plenty moist if you don't overcook it. Call ahead to ask your fishmonger to slice the swordfish thinly for you—just under ½ inch is ideal. If you're good with a knife, you can buy a thick piece and slice it in half horizontally.

You can broil the swordfish, if you prefer—an easier method as you don't have to turn it. Accompany with a salad of tomatoes, cucumbers, red onion, and olives; or with tabouli. If you would rather serve a hot side dish, consider wilted spinach.

Prepare a hot charcoal fire or preheat a gas grill to high. Brush the swordfish steaks on both sides with olive oil and season on both sides with salt and pepper.

In a bowl, whisk together the yogurt, tahini, garlic, lemon juice, 2 tablespoons of the cilantro, 2 tablespoons of the parsley, and salt to taste. The sauce will be thick. Whisk in water until the sauce is thin enough to drizzle, probably ⅓ to ½ cup depending on the thickness of the yogurt and tahini. Taste and adjust the seasoning; you may want more lemon, garlic, or salt. The sauce should be lemony.

Combine the remaining cilantro and parsley to use for a garnish.

Preheat the grill rack well to keep the fish from sticking. Grill the fish, turning once with a spatula, until white throughout, about 2 minutes per side. Because the steaks are so thin, they cook very quickly. Take care not to overcook.

Divide the fish among 6 dinner plates. Spoon the sauce over each steak, dividing it evenly. Sprinkle liberally with sumac, using about ¼ teaspoon per portion. Garnish with the minced cilantro and parsley and serve immediately with the lemon wedges.

Vegetables & Grains

Every season brings fresh-picked vegetables that yogurt complements. In spring, make an asparagus frittata with dill and yogurt cheese (page 101) or a rice pilaf with fresh fava beans and yogurt sauce (page 99). Summer supplies green beans to prepare with Turkish spices and yogurt (page 86), as well as zucchini to grill and garnish with yogurt and feta (page 88). Sweet, dense butternut squash is a highlight of autumn's harvest; try it roasted and dressed with yogurt and pumpkin seeds (page 82). In winter, fettuccine with golden fried onions, yogurt, and poppy seeds (page 98) will introduce you to yogurt in one of its less familiar roles, as part of a delectable pasta sauce.

Roasted Butternut Squash *with* Yogurt & Toasted Pumpkin Seeds

SERVES 4 TO 6

1 butternut squash with a long, straight neck (about 3 pounds)

2 tablespoons extra-virgin olive oil, or more as needed

Kosher or sea salt and freshly ground black pepper

¾ cup plain yogurt

1 small clove garlic, grated or finely minced (see note, page 88)

2 tablespoons store-bought toasted and salted pumpkin seeds

2 to 3 tablespoons coarsely chopped cilantro, for garnish

Medium-hot coarsely ground red pepper such as Maraş or Aleppo pepper (see note), or hot paprika, for garnish

MARAŞ AND ALEPPO PEPPER

Aleppo pepper is from Syria (though also grown in Turkey), and Maraş pepper is from Turkey, but both of these coarsely ground red peppers have a fruity, earthy flavor and a medium-low to medium level of heat. Keep in a tightly sealed jar in the refrigerator or freezer up to 6 months. To locate them, see Resources, page 135.

I roast thick slices of butternut squash until they caramelize a bit on the bottom, and then serve them browned side up. A generous drizzle of tangy yogurt balances their natural sweetness, while toasted pumpkin seeds add crunch. Kabocha squash, with its dense, creamy flesh, is another good choice, but its hard rind and rounded shape make it more challenging to peel. Serve the squash with rice or bulgur pilaf, or pair with pork chops or sausages. To make a more substantial dish, remove some Mexican-style chorizo from its casing, brown in a skillet, and spoon over the top.

Preheat an oven to 400°F. Line a heavy rimmed baking sheet with parchment paper.

Using a cleaver or heavy chef's knife, slice off the stem end of the squash. Cut the squash crosswise at the point where the straight neck connects to the bulbous base, where the seed cavity is. Reserve the base for soup or another use.

Set the neck on a work surface, stem end up, and peel with a cleaver or chef's knife by slicing from top to bottom all the way around the squash. Remove all traces of skin and any greenish flesh under the skin. Cut the pared neck in half lengthwise, and then slice each half into half-moons about ½ inch wide. Put the sliced squash in a bowl and add enough olive oil to coat the slices lightly. Season with salt and pepper. Toss with your hands to coat the squash with the oil and distribute the seasonings. Arrange the squash slices on the baking sheet. Bake until tender and beginning to caramelize on the bottom, about 45 minutes.

While the squash roasts, in a small bowl whisk together the yogurt, garlic, and salt to taste. Keep the garlic flavor subtle; you may not need the entire clove.

Using a spatula, carefully transfer the squash slices to a serving platter, flipping them so the caramelized bottom side is up. Spoon the yogurt over the top. Garnish with the pumpkin seeds, cilantro, and a few shakes of red pepper.

Spinach *with* Brown Butter, Yogurt & Dukka

SERVES 4 AS A FIRST COURSE, 6 AS A SIDE DISH

1½ cups plain drained yogurt (page 22)

1 to 2 cloves garlic, grated or finely minced (see note, page 88)

Kosher or sea salt

3 large bunches fresh spinach, enough to yield 1½ pounds (4 packed quarts) of stemmed leaves

3 tablespoons unsalted butter

3 tablespoons dukka (see recipe introduction)

Medium-hot coarsely ground red pepper such as Aleppo or Maraş pepper (see note, page 82), or hot paprika, for garnish

Skillet Flatbread (page 70) or warm pita

If you have never tasted *dukka*, you have a treat in store. Made from finely ground nuts (usually almonds or hazelnuts), sesame seeds, cumin, and coriander—all toasted separately and then combined—*dukka* is used in Egypt, its home base, mostly as a condiment. Diners dip chunks of bread in olive oil, and then in the *dukka*—a snack for the gods. For a quick lunch, sprinkle *dukka* on yogurt with olive oil and accompany with cucumbers and pita chips for dipping. In this recipe, I shower it over buttery spinach and yogurt—a warm first course to scoop up with flatbread or a side dish for grilled lamb. Look for *dukka* in well-stocked spice shops or see Resources (page 135).

Whisk together the yogurt, garlic, and salt to taste. Cover and let stand at room temperature for 1 hour.

Remove thick spinach stems; if they are slim and tender, you can leave them attached. Wash the leaves well—they can be sandy—and drain. Put the leaves in a large pot with just the wash water clinging to them. Cover and cook over medium heat, tossing with tongs once or twice, until the leaves wilt, about 2 minutes. Drain in a sieve or colander and chill with cold running water. Drain again and squeeze dry.

Melt the butter in a large skillet over medium heat. When the butter begins to brown and smell nutty, add the spinach. Season to taste with salt and toss well with tongs to coat the spinach with the butter. Keep hot.

Divide the yogurt mixture among 4 to 6 plates, spreading it into a pool. Using tongs, divide the spinach among the plates, placing it on top of the yogurt. Scatter ½ tablespoon *dukka* over each portion, and then garnish with a sprinkle of red pepper. Serve with flatbread or pita.

Turkish-Spiced Green Beans with Yogurt

SERVES 4

1 pound green beans, ends trimmed

1 cup plain drained yogurt (page 22) or Greek yogurt (not nonfat)

1 clove garlic, grated or finely minced (see note, page 88)

Kosher or sea salt

3 tablespoons extra-virgin olive oil

1 yellow onion, halved and thinly sliced

1½ teaspoons vadouvan (see recipe introduction)

1 teaspoon medium-hot coarsely ground red pepper such as Maraş or Aleppo pepper (see note, page 82), or hot paprika, plus more for garnish

1 cup peeled, seeded, and diced fresh tomato

¾ cup vegetable stock or chicken broth, plus more as needed

When I first tasted the spiced green beans at Troya, a popular Turkish restaurant in San Francisco, I couldn't imagine what miraculous seasoning made them so delicious. I later learned from the chef that he uses *vadouvan*, a spice blend with Indian and French influences, often referred to as French curry. *Vadouvan* (see Resources, page 135) varies from one maker to the next but typically includes turmeric, cumin, curry leaves, toasted shallots, and garlic. You can substitute curry powder, but the result will not be as intriguing.

At Troya, the beans are blanched first, and then braised with tomato, sautéed onion, and *vadouvan*. A garlicky yogurt sauce softens the spice. Serve with bulgur or rice for a vegetarian meal, or as a side dish with lemony roast chicken.

Bring a large pot of salted water to a boil over high heat. Add the green beans and boil until tender, about 5 minutes. They should be fully cooked, not crunchy. Drain in a sieve or colander and rinse with cold water to stop the cooking. Drain again and let dry.

In a small bowl, whisk together the yogurt, garlic, and salt to taste until creamy.

Heat the oil in a large skillet over medium-low heat. Add the onion and sauté until soft and lightly colored, 8 to 10 minutes. Add the *vadouvan* and red pepper and sauté for 1 minute so the spices lose their raw taste. Add the tomato and a generous pinch of salt. Raise the heat to medium-high and cook, stirring with a wooden spoon, until the tomato collapses into a puree, about 5 minutes, depending on ripeness. Add the stock and simmer over medium heat until the mixture is thick and tasty, about 5 minutes. Add the green beans and another pinch of salt. Toss with tongs to mix well. Simmer gently, adding a splash more stock if necessary to loosen the sauce, until the green beans are hot throughout. Taste and adjust the seasoning. (Beans need a lot of salt.) For best flavor, let them cool in the sauce, and then reheat gently to serve.

Divide the beans among 4 plates. Top each portion with the yogurt sauce, dividing it equally, and another dash of red pepper.

Seared Mushrooms & Shallots in Yogurt *with* Garam Masala

SERVES 4 TO 6

2 cups plain drained yogurt (page 22) or Greek yogurt (not nonfat)

¼ packed cup chopped cilantro

1 large clove garlic, grated or finely minced (see note, page 88)

Kosher or sea salt

3 tablespoons ghee (see note), clarified butter, or vegetable oil

1 pound cremini mushrooms, quartered if large, halved if small

¾ teaspoon freshly ground black pepper

1 teaspoon garam masala

1 cup thinly sliced shallots

GHEE

Indian clarified butter (ghee) has a nutty aroma like brown butter. To make it, slowly melt fresh butter, and then cook until the milk solids fall to the bottom of the pan and begin to brown. Pour off the clear, golden butter on top—ghee—leaving the solids behind. Ghee is useful for sautéing because it can withstand a higher temperature than fresh butter without burning. I use it when I want a dish to have a proper Indian flavor. You can make ghee yourself, but every Indian market carries it. It keeps for weeks in the refrigerator.

High heat is the key to cooking cremini mushrooms successfully. They need to sear briskly to caramelize the exterior, retain their firmness, and seal in the juices. The alternative is a skillet full of limp, steamed mushrooms, and there's no pleasure in that. I like to season the mushrooms with a big pinch of black pepper and garam masala, the fragrant Indian spice blend that almost always includes cinnamon and clove. Folded into thick yogurt with caramelized shallots, the mushrooms make a warm, creamy accompaniment for a grilled steak, veal chop, or chicken breast, or the foundation of a meatless meal with wild rice or farro. I like to use ghee because it doesn't burn easily and has a subtle nutty taste, but vegetable oil will do. If you serve the mushrooms with a pan-seared steak or roast, stir some of the meat juices into the yogurt.

In a large bowl, whisk together the yogurt, cilantro, garlic, and salt to taste.

Heat a large, heavy skillet over high heat. Add 2 tablespoons of the ghee and swirl to coat. Add the mushrooms. Do not stir for 30 to 60 seconds to allow the mushrooms to brown, then give a quick stir or shake. Season with salt and ½ teaspoon of the black pepper. Sear until the mushrooms are richly browned all over and tender, about 5 minutes, stirring just enough to prevent scorching and reducing the heat if needed. (If you stir too much or cook too slowly, the mushrooms will release liquid and steam rather than sear.) Add the garam masala and cook about 1 minute longer, then fold the mushrooms into the yogurt.

Let the skillet cool slightly, then add the remaining ghee and return to medium-low heat. Add the shallots and season with salt and the remaining black pepper. Cook the shallots, stirring often, until they begin to caramelize, about 10 minutes. Use a wooden spoon to scrape up any softening mushroom residue on the bottom of the skillet. Scrape the shallots into the yogurt mixture and fold in.

If the skillet still has some browned residue on the bottom, return it to medium heat and add a few splashes of water. Simmer briskly, scraping with a wooden spoon, until the residue dissolves and the liquid reduces to about 1 tablespoon. Fold into the yogurt. Taste and adjust the seasoning, and then serve immediately.

Grilled Zucchini *with* Yogurt Sauce, Feta, Lemon & Dill

SERVES 4

¾ cup plain yogurt

1 large clove garlic, grated or finely minced (see note)

Kosher or sea salt

6 small zucchini (about 1¼ pounds), halved lengthwise

Extra-virgin olive oil, for brushing

3 ounces feta cheese (about ¾ cup), chilled

2 tablespoons chopped fresh dill

Grated zest of 1 small lemon

Medium-hot coarsely ground red pepper such as Aleppo or Maraş pepper (see note, page 82), or hot paprika

GRATING VERSUS MINCING GARLIC

I typically use a Microplane, a rasp-style grater available at kitchenware stores, when adding garlic to yogurt. You can also mince the garlic finely with a knife, but I find that grated garlic infuses the yogurt better. It practically dissolves, so you don't perceive any little bits of garlic in the yogurt. However, for a dish with sautéed garlic, such as Orzo with Spicy Lamb, Chickpeas & Yogurt (page 72), I prefer to mince it, as grated garlic produces too strong a flavor.

If you are grilling lamb, chicken, sausage, or salmon, make some room on the grill for halved zucchini. When they're richly browned, nestle the zucchini on a bed of garlicky yogurt, crumble feta over the top, and then shower them with lemon zest and dill. For eye appeal, use a mix of summer squashes—green and golden zucchini and the flat scallopini types. At my house, we like this dish so much that we often dispense with the meat and just have grilled zucchini for our dinner, with bulgur, couscous, or rice.

Prepare a medium-hot charcoal fire or preheat a gas grill to medium-high.

In a small bowl, whisk together the yogurt, garlic, and salt to taste. Spread the yogurt sauce on a serving platter large enough to hold all the zucchini in one layer.

Brush the zucchini on both sides with olive oil and season all over with salt. Place cut side down on the grill and cook until nicely browned, and then turn and finish cooking on the skin side until they are tender, about 10 minutes total. Transfer the zucchini to the platter, placing them on the yogurt sauce cut side up. Finely crumble the feta over the zucchini. (This is easier to do if the feta is cold.) Combine the dill and lemon zest and scatter over the zucchini, and then sprinkle generously with red pepper. Serve immediately.

Alsatian Pizza with Onions & Pancetta

(Tarte Flambée)

SERVES 2 TO 4

Pizza Dough (recipe follows) or 1 pound
store-bought pizza dough,
at room temperature

1 tablespoon all-purpose flour, plus more
for dusting

1 tablespoon extra-virgin olive oil

½ large yellow onion, thinly sliced

Kosher or sea salt and freshly
ground black pepper

¾ cup plain drained yogurt (page 22)
or Greek yogurt (not nonfat)

1 large egg yolk

A few scrapings of whole nutmeg or pinch
of ground nutmeg

Fine semolina, for the pizza peel

3 to 4 ounces pancetta, cut into ¼-inch
dice, at room temperature

1 tablespoon chopped Italian parsley

One of my favorite vacation memories is of the boisterous Alsatian pizzeria where my husband and I first encountered *tarte flambée* ("flaming tart"), also known as *flammekueche*. We sat at long communal tables and had what everyone else was having: *crudités* to start—vinaigrette-dressed salads of grated carrots and celery root—and then slabs of sizzling Alsatian pizza from a wood-fired oven. Traditional *tarte flambée* has a base of crème fraîche or fresh pot cheese, with a topping of onions and bacon. I have substituted yogurt and like the contrast of its tang against the sweet onions.

The unusual pizza-cooking technique that I suggest below—preheating the pizza stone under the broiler and then broiling the pizza for the first few minutes—is a procedure I developed to compensate for my home oven, which can't be coaxed any hotter than 475°F. Preheating the stone under the broiler ensures that the bottom of the pizza will get crisp, and the initial broiling of the pizza browns the top. I turn off the broiler element as soon as the exposed dough is nicely colored and just starting to blister and then complete the cooking at the hottest possible baking temperature. This method works like a dream for me, but every home oven is a little universe of its own. You may need to deviate from my suggested timings. Note that you need a pizza stone or pizza tiles large enough to accommodate a 14-inch pizza.

Position a rack in the upper third of the oven. Set a pizza stone on the rack and preheat the oven to its highest setting for at least 45 minutes to heat the stone thoroughly.

If using homemade Pizza Dough: Prepare the recipe through the second rise. Punch down the dough and turn it out onto a lightly floured surface. Shape into a ball. Dust the top with flour and invert a bowl over the dough. Let rest for 30 minutes. If using store-bought dough, follow the package directions to prepare it for baking.

About 20 minutes before baking, turn on the broiler to heat the top surface of the baking stone.

continued

Warm the olive oil in a small skillet over medium heat. Add the onion, season with salt and pepper, and sauté until softened but not colored, about 5 minutes. Transfer to a plate.

In a bowl, whisk together the yogurt, egg yolk, 1 tablespoon flour, nutmeg, ½ teaspoon salt, and several grinds of black pepper.

Generously dust a pizza peel or rimless baking sheet with semolina.

Using floured fingertips, flatten the pizza dough into a round about 10 inches in diameter. Now you need to stretch it further by hand, until it is about 14 inches in diameter. (A rolling pin forces too much air out, and the dough wants to stick to it.) For me, the easiest stretching method is to drape the flattened dough across the back of my floured knuckles, and then rotate the dough, gradually moving my hands farther apart as the dough stretches. Don't be concerned if the dough isn't perfectly round—a misshapen pizza has handmade charm.

Transfer the stretched dough to the prepared peel. Working quickly, top the dough with the yogurt mixture, spreading it almost to the rim using a rubber spatula, and then scatter the onion on top. Dot the surface with the pancetta.

Slide the pizza onto the preheated stone. Broil until the rim is puffed and golden brown, 3 to 4 minutes. (Every broiler is different, so monitor carefully to prevent scorching.) Turn off the broiler and return the oven thermostat to the highest setting. Continue baking until the pizza bottom is fully cooked and lightly browned, about 5 minutes longer. Transfer the pizza to a cutting board, sprinkle with the parsley, and cut into wedges to serve.

Alternate baking method: If you don't have an oven with a broiler element, you can also bake the pizza from start to finish. Preheat the oven to its highest setting, and bake the pizza at that temperature for the entire time. It will take a few minutes longer than the partial-broiling method.

Pizza Dough

MAKES APPROXIMATELY 1 POUND OF DOUGH, ENOUGH FOR ONE 15-INCH PIZZA

1½ teaspoons active dry yeast

¾ cup warm water (105°F to 110°F)

1 tablespoon extra-virgin olive oil

About 1¾ cups unbleached all-purpose flour

1 teaspoon kosher or sea salt

Sprinkle the yeast over the warm water in a large bowl. Let stand for 2 minutes to soften, and then whisk with a fork to blend. Let stand for 10 minutes to proof; the yeast should begin to bloom on the surface. Whisk in the olive oil.

In a bowl, whisk together 1½ cups of the flour and the salt. Add the flour mixture to the water and stir with a wooden spoon until the dough clears the sides of the bowl. Transfer to a lightly floured work surface and knead until soft and smooth, about 5 minutes, adding as much of the remaining ¼ cup flour as needed to keep the dough from sticking to the work surface or your hands. Shape the dough into a ball and place it in a lightly oiled bowl. Turn to coat the surface of the dough with oil. Cover the bowl with plastic wrap and let rise 2 hours.

Punch down the dough, and reshape it into a ball; re-cover the bowl and let the dough rise again for 4 hours.

Warm Chickpeas *with* Toasted Pita, Pine Nuts & Yogurt Sauce

SERVES 4

¼ cup pine nuts

2 whole-grain pita bread rounds

2 cups plain yogurt (not nonfat)

1 to 2 cloves garlic, grated or finely minced (see note, page 88)

1 teaspoon finely minced fresh mint

Kosher or sea salt and freshly ground black pepper

3 cups Boiled Chickpeas (recipe follows) or 3 cups canned chickpeas, drained and rinsed

1 cup broth from Boiled Chickpeas or canned chicken or vegetable broth

1 tablespoon unsalted butter

½ teaspoon medium-hot coarsely ground red pepper such as Aleppo or Maraş pepper (see note, page 82), or hot paprika

2 tablespoons chopped cilantro

Ground sumac, for garnish

Stale bread has inspired some of the world's tastiest dishes, including this one from the Arab kitchen. In Lebanon, Syria, and Egypt, frugal cooks layer their tired flatbread with moist ingredients, like boiled chickpeas or chicken, and big dollops of garlicky yogurt. The dry bread softens quickly in the juicy layers, becoming like pasta in a creamy lasagna. I use toasted whole wheat pita, and I like to cook my own chickpeas so I have a flavorful broth for moistening. On top of the snow white yogurt: a flourish of fried pine nuts, chiles, sumac, and cilantro. For a more robust dish, add a couple layers of shredded poached chicken or browned ground lamb.

Preheat an oven to 325°F. Toast the pine nuts in a pie tin or on a baking sheet until they are evenly golden brown, about 5 minutes, shaking them to redistribute partway through. Let cool.

Using your hands, carefully tear each pita in half along the "equator" to yield half-moons, each with a pocket. Gently open the half-moons and separate the pockets at the rounded edge so that you have eight half-moon pieces. Under a preheated broiler or in a toaster oven, toast the pita on both sides until crisp; watch carefully to avoid scorching. Let cool, and then break into pieces about the size of tortilla chips.

In a bowl, whisk together the yogurt, garlic, mint, and salt and pepper to taste.

Put the chickpeas and broth in a saucepan and bring to a simmer over medium heat. Cover and adjust the heat to maintain a gentle simmer.

Put half of the toasted pita in a serving dish. Moisten with about ⅓ cup of the hot broth. Add half of the chickpeas, lifting them out with a slotted spoon and scattering them over the pita.

Spoon half of the yogurt over the chickpeas. Repeat the layering: toasted pita, hot broth, chickpeas, and yogurt.

In a small saucepan, melt the butter over medium heat. Add the red pepper and sauté until its fragrance rises, less than 1 minute. Add the pine nuts and stir to coat with butter. When the butter sizzles and foams, spoon the pine nuts and all the butter over the yogurt. Garnish with the cilantro and a shower of sumac and serve immediately.

continued

Boiled Chickpeas

MAKES ABOUT 7½ CUPS COOKED CHICKPEAS AND 6 CUPS BROTH

1 pound dried chickpeas, soaked overnight in enough water to cover generously

3 cloves garlic, peeled and halved

1 dozen black peppercorns

1 whole clove

1 onion, peeled and halved

1 large celery rib, cut into 4 pieces

2 carrots, cut into large chunks

2 bay leaves

Kosher or sea salt

You can also cook the chickpeas in a pressure cooker, following the manufacturer's instructions. For presoaked beans, pressure-cook for 12 minutes, and then remove from the heat and let the pressure cooker cool before releasing the lid. Use leftover chickpeas in salads or in soups, such as the Chicken Soup with Toasted Pasta, Chickpeas & Yogurt (page 55).

Drain the chickpeas and put them in a large pot with 2 quarts of cold water. Bring to a simmer over medium heat, skimming off any foam. Wrap the garlic, peppercorns, and clove in a cheesecloth sachet or enclose in a tea ball. When the chickpeas stop generating foam, add the onion, celery, carrots, bay leaves, and sachet. Return to a simmer, cover, and adjust the heat to maintain a gentle simmer. Cook until the chickpeas are fully tender, about 1½ hours. Season with salt and let cool in the cooking liquid. When cool, discard the onion, carrots, celery, and bay leaves, and remove the sachet. Refrigerate the chickpeas in their cooking broth. They will keep for about 5 days.

Warm Chard Ribs *in* Yogurt *with* Toasted Walnuts, Cilantro & Cumin

SERVES 4

1 cup plain yogurt, at room temperature

2 tablespoons finely chopped cilantro, plus more for garnish

1 clove garlic, grated or finely minced (see note, page 88)

Scant ¼ teaspoon toasted and ground cumin seeds (see note, page 45)

Kosher or sea salt and freshly ground black pepper

4 cups ½-inch-diced white chard ribs

⅓ cup toasted and coarsely chopped walnuts (see page 29)

When I prepare Swiss chard, I always slice the leaves off the ribs because the leaves cook faster. Typically, after cooking them separately, I'll reunite ribs and leaves. But when I find chard with particularly broad and pristine ribs, I'll cook and serve the ribs on their own with butter and Parmesan cheese or in this warm yogurt sauce. I may serve the cooked leaves alongside or at another meal.

To separate the ribs from the leaves, hold a leaf upside down by the stem. Using a sharp knife, slice down along both sides of the rib to cut it loose. I think white-ribbed chard has the most delicate flavor, but you can use yellow or red ribs here if you like. Use drained or Greek yogurt if you want a thicker sauce. Serve with roast chicken or slices of garlicky roast lamb.

In a serving bowl large enough to hold the chard ribs, whisk together the yogurt, cilantro, garlic, cumin, and salt and pepper to taste.

Bring a large pot of salted water to a boil over high heat. Add the chard ribs and boil until tender, 5 to 8 minutes. Drain in a sieve or colander, shake dry, and let cool for 2 minutes so their heat does not curdle the yogurt. Fold the warm chard ribs into the yogurt along with the walnuts. Taste for seasoning. Garnish with more cilantro and serve immediately.

Fettuccine *with* Fried Onions, Yogurt & Poppy Seeds

SERVES 6

1½ cups plain whole-milk yogurt,
at room temperature

1 large clove garlic, grated or finely minced
(see note, page 88)

1 teaspoon dried spearmint

Kosher or sea salt

¼ cup ghee (see note, page 87)
or clarified butter

1½ pounds yellow onions, halved and thinly
sliced from stem to root end

Medium-hot coarsely ground red pepper
such as Aleppo or Maraş pepper (see note,
page 82), or freshly ground black pepper

1 pound dried fettuccine or linguine

2 tablespoons poppy seeds

2 tablespoons minced Italian parsley

There's nothing Italian about this dish except for the pasta. The warm yogurt sauce and fried-onion topping come from the Eastern Mediterranean. Some similar recipes include lemony sumac to counter the sweet onions, but I prefer the heat of chiles or freshly ground black pepper. Be sure to use whole-milk yogurt or the sauce may break when you add the hot pasta. Ghee, the nutty clarified butter that every Indian market stocks, gives the fried onions a lovely brown-butter flavor, but you can use clarified butter instead. Fresh butter would burn.

In a bowl large enough to hold all the cooked pasta, whisk together the yogurt, garlic, mint, and 1 teaspoon salt. Let stand in a warm place, such as near the stove, or set the bowl in a larger bowl of warm water. Put 6 pasta bowls in a low oven to warm.

Bring 6 quarts of well-salted water to a boil over high heat.

Melt the ghee in a large skillet over high heat. Add the onions and season well with salt. Add 1 teaspoon red pepper or several grinds of black pepper and sauté briskly until the onions are deeply browned and crisp in spots, about 10 minutes. Reduce the heat gradually to keep the onions from scorching, but they should fry, not sweat. Taste when they are about half done and add more red pepper or black pepper, if needed. The onions should be spicy because the yogurt is bland. Keep warm over low heat.

Cook the pasta in the boiling water until al dente. Set aside about 1 cup of the hot pasta water for "insurance." Drain the pasta and transfer it to the bowl with the yogurt. Add 1 tablespoon of the poppy seeds. Toss well using tongs. Thin with the reserved hot water if needed. Divide among the 6 warmed bowls. Top with the warm onions, dividing them equally, and garnish each serving with some of the remaining 1 tablespoon poppy seeds and the parsley. Serve immediately.

Rice Pilaf *with* Fava Beans & Yogurt Sauce

SERVES 4

YOGURT DILL SAUCE

½ cup plain yogurt

1 large clove garlic, grated or finely minced (see note, page 88)

1 tablespoon chopped fresh dill

Kosher or sea salt

PILAF WITH FAVA BEANS

1 cup basmati rice

2 pounds fresh fava beans, shelled

1½ cups chicken or vegetable broth (if canned, use equal parts broth and water)

2 tablespoons unsalted butter

½ cup thinly sliced green onions

My friend Sotiris Kitrilakis, formerly a Greek food exporter, lives on the lovely Greek island of Zakynthos in the Ionian Sea. Like me, he has simple tastes and eats largely from his own garden and the farmers' market. Unlike me, he has shepherds for neighbors, so he has a ready supply of thick sheep's-milk yogurt. In spring, when fresh peas are in season, he makes this delicate pilaf and serves it with yogurt alongside. I have replaced the peas with fava beans because I grow favas more successfully, but substitute peas if you prefer. Obviously, they don't require blanching and peeling, as favas do, so you can omit those steps.

Serve this pilaf as a side dish with lamb or as a meatless main course with some braised carrots or wilted spinach. You can replace the rice with coarse bulgur if you like. The cooking time is the same.

To make the sauce: In a bowl, whisk together the yogurt, garlic, dill, and salt to taste.

To make the pilaf: Put the rice in a bowl with enough water to cover it by 2 inches. Swish with your fingers to dislodge starch, and then carefully pour off the cloudy water. Repeat several times, until the water is mostly clear. If you have time, cover the rice with cold water and let it soak for 1 hour. Drain the rice in a sieve and shake well to remove all excess water.

Bring a large pot of water to a boil and have ready a bowl of ice water. Blanch the fava beans in the boiling water for 1 minute, and then drain and immediately transfer to the ice water to stop the cooking. When the beans are cold, drain again. To peel the beans, pierce the skin with your fingernail. The peeled bean will slip out easily.

Bring the broth to a simmer in a small saucepan. Season with salt. Melt 1 tablespoon of the butter in a medium saucepan over medium heat. Add the drained rice and sauté, stirring constantly, until it just begins to color, 2 to 3 minutes. Add the hot broth, bring to a simmer, then cover the pan and reduce the heat to low. Cook for 15 minutes, then wrap a

continued

clean dish towel around the lid to absorb steam, replace the lid on the pan, and remove from the heat. Let stand for 10 minutes.

Melt the remaining 1 tablespoon butter in a small saucepan over medium heat. Add the green onions and sauté until softened, about 1 minute. Add the peeled fava beans and season with salt. Add 2 tablespoons water and bring to a simmer. Cover and reduce the heat to maintain a gentle simmer. Cook until the favas are tender, about 5 minutes, and then uncover, raise the heat, and simmer until there is no liquid remaining in the pan.

Transfer the rice to a serving bowl and fluff it with a fork to separate the grains. Fold in the fava beans and toss gently with a fork to blend them in without breaking the rice grains. Serve immediately with the yogurt sauce on the side.

Asparagus Frittata *with* Yogurt Cheese

SERVES 4

1 dozen slender asparagus

6 large eggs, lightly beaten

¼ cup grated pecorino romano or Parmigiano-Reggiano cheese

2 packed tablespoons minced fresh dill

1 teaspoon kosher or sea salt

Freshly ground black pepper

2 tablespoons extra-virgin olive oil

½ cup minced green onions, white and pale green parts only

¼ cup yogurt cheese (page 23)

When this frittata is about half done, I spoon small dollops of creamy yogurt cheese on top. The egg sets around the yogurt cheese, trapping it in little pools. On another occasion, you could substitute sliced leeks or artichoke hearts for the asparagus. I enjoy a frittata most when it is warm or at room temperature, not hot. I even like it cold in a baguette sandwich with some soft lettuce.

Preheat an oven to 375°F and position a rack in the center.

Grasping an asparagus spear in both hands, bend gently so that it breaks at the point where the spear becomes tough. Discard the tough end. Repeat with the remaining asparagus. Cut off the asparagus tips and set aside. Slice the remaining part of the spears on the diagonal into ½-inch-wide pieces.

In a bowl, whisk together the eggs, cheese, dill, ½ teaspoon of the salt, and several grinds of black pepper.

Heat the olive oil in a 10-inch nonstick skillet over medium-low heat. Add the green onions and the sliced asparagus. Season with the remaining ½ teaspoon salt and several grinds of black pepper. Cook, stirring often, until the asparagus pieces have softened slightly, 5 to 10 minutes. Add the egg mixture. Cook for about 5 minutes, and then scatter the asparagus tips on the surface, which will still be moist. Place teaspoon-size dollops of the yogurt cheese on the surface, spreading them evenly and using it all. Continue cooking until the frittata is almost set but still slightly moist, about 5 minutes longer. Transfer to the oven and bake until the surface is just firm to the touch, 3 to 5 minutes longer. Slide the frittata out of the skillet onto a cutting board and let cool slightly. Serve warm, not hot, in wedges.

Desserts

Creamy, tangy, and compatible with fruit, yogurt inspires
endless desserts. It adds a tender crumb to a cake (page 122) and
a lemony lightness to sorbet (page 121) and panna cotta (page 116).
Paired creatively with each season's most enticing fruit—from
mangoes to peaches to pomegranates to quinces—yogurt delivers
a year's worth of luscious finales.

Yogurt Parfait *with* Peaches & Peanut Brittle

SERVES 6

3 cups plain drained yogurt (page 22)

2 tablespoons plus 2 teaspoons sugar

⅛ teaspoon vanilla extract

4 ounces peanut brittle

2 ripe peaches or nectarines, peeled and cut into thin wedges

Any recipe that justifies buying peanut brittle is a keeper in my estimation. Hard, crunchy almond nougat—not the chewy type—could replace the brittle, or substitute granola if you're feeling more abstemious.

In a bowl, whisk together the yogurt, 2 tablespoons of the sugar, and the vanilla. Refrigerate until ready to serve.

Put the peanut brittle between 2 sheets of waxed paper or parchment paper. Using a rolling pin or mallet, crush the brittle until it is about the size of small pebbles. The pieces will be uneven in size, which is fine.

In a bowl, toss the sliced peaches with the remaining 2 teaspoons sugar. Let stand for 15 minutes to draw out the juices.

In a glass serving dish or in 6 individual parfait glasses or wineglasses, make a layer of yogurt, followed by peaches, and then brittle, using half of each. Repeat the layers with the remaining yogurt, peaches, and peanut brittle. Serve immediately.

Yogurt *with* Mango, Toasted Coconut & Cashews

SERVES 4

½ cup unsweetened shredded coconut

8 teaspoons honey or agave nectar

2 cups plain drained yogurt (page 22)

1⅓ cups diced ripe mango

6 tablespoons roasted salted cashews, coarsely chopped

If you have ever enjoyed mango lassi, the Indian blender drink, you know how compatible mangoes and yogurt are. This dessert makes the same point in another way, with layers of creamy yogurt, ripe mango, toasted coconut, and salted nuts. You'll find the best, most aromatic mangoes in markets in May and June. Don't judge by color alone. Lift the mango to your nose, and if it doesn't have a seductive tropical fragrance, put it back.

Preheat an oven to 325°F. Spread the coconut on a baking sheet and bake until golden, about 4 minutes, stirring once halfway through to help the coconut toast evenly. Do not allow it to become dark brown or it will be bitter. Let cool.

If the honey is stiff and crystalline, warm it in a small saucepan over low heat until it liquefies enough to drizzle.

Put ⅓ cup of the yogurt in each of 4 parfait glasses or compote dishes. Top each serving with 1 teaspoon honey, ⅓ cup mango, and 1 tablespoon toasted coconut. Divide the remaining yogurt among the 4 glasses. Top each portion with 1½ tablespoons cashews, 1 tablespoon coconut, and 1 teaspoon honey. Serve immediately.

Warm Baked Figs *with* Pernod, Candied Walnuts & Yogurt

SERVES 4

½ cup Pernod or other anise-flavored spirit, plus more as needed

1 dozen Black Mission or other dark-skinned figs, stemmed and halved (about ½ pound)

1 tablespoon plus 1 teaspoon sugar

2 cups plain drained yogurt (page 22)

⅓ cup Candied Walnuts (recipe follows), coarsely crumbled

I enjoy figs and anise together in any format, from yeast breads to ice cream. For this dish, I use Pernod to perfume the figs, but you could substitute Pastis, a similar French anise spirit, or Greek ouzo. Sambuca, the Italian anise liqueur, would also work, but it is sweeter so I would cut back on the recipe's sugar. Purple-skinned figs aren't essential but they produce a gorgeous amethyst syrup.

Preheat an oven to 425°F. Choose a baking dish just large enough to hold the halved figs in one layer. Pour the ½ cup Pernod into the baking dish. Place the figs in the dish, skin side down. Sprinkle the surface of the figs with the sugar. Bake for 10 minutes, then baste them with the juices and return them to the oven until the figs soften completely and the juices are reduced to about 2 tablespoons, about 10 minutes longer. Remove from the oven and let cool for 5 minutes.

Divide the yogurt among 4 compote dishes. Place the warm baked figs on top, dividing them equally. Spoon the dark, syrupy juices over the figs. (If the juices reduced a little too much and you have less than 2 tablespoons, thin with a splash of Pernod and stir with a wooden spoon until smooth.) Top with the crumbled candied walnuts. Serve immediately.

Candied Walnuts

MAKES ABOUT 1½ CUPS

¼ cup granulated sugar

¼ cup packed light brown sugar

¼ teaspoon kosher or sea salt

¼ teaspoon vanilla extract

1½ cups walnut halves

Put a sheet of parchment paper near the stove. In a saucepan or skillet large enough to accommodate the walnuts, combine the granulated sugar, brown sugar, and salt. Mix with your fingers until well blended, with no remaining lumps of brown sugar. Cook over medium heat, stirring with a wooden spoon, until the sugar completely liquefies and forms a dark liquid caramel. (It will clump before it melts.) Watch carefully and do not allow it to burn; lower the heat if necessary. When the caramel is completely molten, stir in the vanilla, which will cause the caramel to hiss and sizzle; continue stirring until smooth again.

Working quickly, add the nuts to the caramel and stir to coat them as evenly as possible—they will clump—and then pour the stiff mass onto the parchment paper. Be careful not to touch the hot nuts; a caramel burn is nasty. Don't worry if some of the caramel stays behind in the pan. For ease of cleaning, immediately put the pan in the sink and add water. Let the nuts cool completely, and then break them into smaller clumps and store in an airtight jar. Candied walnuts will keep for at least 1 month.

Yogurt *with* Blueberries, Hazelnuts & Maple Syrup

SERVES 4

¼ cup hazelnuts

1 pint fresh blueberries

4 tablespoons maple syrup

2 cups plain drained yogurt (page 22)

No blueberries compare to wild Oregon blueberries, no hazelnuts to Oregon hazelnuts, no maple syrup to the burnt-amber maple syrup from Oregon. These firm opinions come from my husband, who was largely raised in—you guessed it—Oregon.

Preheat an oven to 350°F. Bring a small pot of water to a boil over high heat and add the hazelnuts. Boil for 30 seconds, and then drain. Immediately wrap the hot hazelnuts in a dish towel and rub them in the folds of the towel to remove the brown skin. Some bits of skin may cling to the nuts, but remove as much as you can. Put the skinned hazelnuts on a baking sheet and bake until golden brown and fragrant, 5 to 8 minutes. Let cool, and then chop very coarsely.

Set aside ⅔ cup of the blueberries. Put the remaining blueberries in a saucepan with 2 tablespoons plus 2 teaspoons of the maple syrup. Cover and cook over medium-low heat, stirring occasionally, until the berries collapse completely and release their dark purple juice, about 5 minutes. Remove from the heat and stir in the reserved blueberries. The mixture will be thin. Transfer to a small bowl, cover, and chill.

At serving time, divide the yogurt among 4 parfait glasses or wineglasses. Top each portion with some of the chilled blueberries and hazelnuts, dividing them equally, and pour 1 teaspoon of the remaining maple syrup over each. Serve immediately.

Poached Quinces *with* Yogurt & Pistachios

SERVES 6

2 cups water

1 cup sugar

2 strips orange zest, removed using
a vegetable peeler (colored part only)

1 strip lemon zest, removed using
a vegetable peeler (colored part only)

2 whole cardamom pods

2 ripe quinces, about 8 ounces each

½ teaspoon rose water, or more to taste

3 tablespoons shelled raw pistachios

3 cups plain drained yogurt (page 22)

A ripe quince looks something like a knobby, misshapen Golden Delicious apple, with firm, pale yellow flesh and a heady sweet-apple scent. But don't be tempted to take a bite. The tannic flesh is not palatable until cooked, typically with a substantial amount of sugar. Be patient with quince. As it cooks, the flesh changes from soft yellow to pale salmon to the color of ruby grapefruit, and its intense, exotic flavor emerges. A few drops of rose water heighten its potent perfume. Mellow yogurt is the perfect complement. Cooked quince keeps well, so you can prepare it up to 3 days ahead. Look for the fruit at produce markets and farmers' markets in the fall.

In a medium saucepan, combine the water, sugar, orange zest, and lemon zest. Smack the cardamom pods lightly with the side of a knife blade to crack them slightly, and add them to the pot. Bring to a simmer, stirring to dissolve the sugar. Adjust the heat to maintain a gentle simmer.

Peel, quarter, and core the quinces. Cut each quarter into approximately ½-inch dice. Add the quince to the simmering sugar syrup. Cover and adjust the heat to maintain a gentle simmer. Cook until the quince turns a deep rose color and becomes very tender, about 2 hours. Uncover and simmer until the syrup has reduced to ½ cup. Remove from the heat and let the quince cool in the syrup. Stir in the rose water. Remove the citrus peels and cardamom pods. Transfer the quince and all the syrup to a lidded container. Cover and refrigerate until chilled.

Preheat an oven to 325°F. Toast the pistachios in a pie tin until fragrant, 5 to 7 minutes. Let cool; they will become crisp as they cool. Chop coarsely.

Set aside half of the quince mixture. Divide the remainder among 6 parfait glasses or Martini glasses. Top each portion with ½ cup yogurt. Spoon the reserved quince on top of the yogurt, dividing it equally. Scatter the pistachios on top and serve immediately.

Yogurt Parfait

with

Cinnamon-Apple Compote & Granola

SERVES 4

APPLE COMPOTE

¾ pound Golden Delicious apples
(2 medium)

¼ cup light brown sugar

¼ cup water

1 tablespoon freshly squeezed lemon juice

Pinch of ground cinnamon

2 cups plain drained yogurt (page 22)

2 tablespoons maple syrup, or to taste

1 cup granola

Is it breakfast or is it dessert? If you like a sweet start to the day, you'll appreciate this wholesome alternative to pastry. For a quick breakfast, make the apple compote the night before so you can assemble the parfaits in an instant. Use your own homemade granola or bring home several selections from your supermarket's bulk bins. Then you can have a different version every morning.

With its layers of fruit and crunch and cream, this parfait also makes a luscious dessert. Ideally, assemble it shortly before serving so the granola stays crisp. Golden Delicious apples work well here, as they hold their shape when cooked and have a good balance between acidity and sweetness. A tart variety like Granny Smith will be less pleasing.

To make the apple compote: Peel, quarter, and core the apples. Slice each quarter thinly crosswise. Put the apple slices in a wide saucepan with the sugar, water, lemon juice, and cinnamon. Bring to a simmer, stirring to dissolve the sugar. Cover and adjust the heat to maintain a gentle simmer. Watch carefully and lower the heat, if necessary, to keep the syrup from boiling over. Cook until the apple slices are tender but still hold their shape, 5 to 7 minutes. If there is still liquid remaining in the pan, uncover and simmer until it evaporates. Taste and add a pinch more cinnamon if desired. Let cool, and then chill thoroughly.

At serving time, put the yogurt in a bowl and whisk in the maple syrup.

In each of 4 parfait glasses or wineglasses, make layers as follows: ¼ cup of the yogurt, one-eighth of the apple compote, 2 tablespoons of the granola, one-eighth of the apple compote, ¼ cup yogurt, and 2 tablespoons granola. Serve immediately.

Yogurt Mousse *with* Orange Marmalade & Toasted Almonds

SERVES 6

2 cups plain drained yogurt (page 22)

1 cup heavy cream

½ cup sugar

½ teaspoon kosher or sea salt

½ vanilla bean, split lengthwise

1 teaspoon powdered unflavored gelatin

¼ cup sliced almonds

6 scant tablespoons orange marmalade
(see recipe introduction)

This fluffy mousse tastes like a luscious cheesecake without the crust, and it makes an elegant do-ahead dessert. Bill Corbett, the executive pastry chef for the Absinthe Group in San Francisco, shared the recipe, which I have adapted slightly. Bill suggests other toppings as well, including granola, fresh berries, fresh orange segments, or cookie crumbs.

Of course, you can substitute another kind of fruit preserves for the marmalade, but I like the bitter edge that marmalade contributes. However, I make my own and it contains no added pectin. Many commercial marmalades have pectin added and are consequently quite stiff. If the marmalade you choose is stiff, warm it in a saucepan with a few drops of water, stirring until it liquefies. Then give it a few pulses in a food processor to chop up the thick pieces of orange rind.

Put the yogurt in a large bowl.

In a small saucepan, stir together ¼ cup of the cream with the sugar and salt. Using the tip of a paring knife, scrape the vanilla bean seeds into the mixture and add the pod. Sprinkle the gelatin over the mixture and let stand for 1 minute to soften. Bring to a simmer over medium heat, whisking constantly to dissolve the sugar and gelatin. Simmer for 2 minutes, whisking. Strain through a sieve directly into the yogurt. Stir to blend. Cover the bowl and refrigerate for about 30 minutes.

In another bowl, whip the remaining ¾ cup cream to soft peaks. Gently fold the whipped cream into the yogurt mixture. Divide among 6 glasses. Cover each glass with plastic wrap and refrigerate until set, at least 2 hours. You can make the mousse up to 8 hours ahead.

Preheat an oven to 325°F. Toast the almonds on a baking sheet or in a pie tin until golden brown, stirring once or twice so they cook evenly, about 5 minutes. Let cool.

To serve, put a scant 1 tablespoon marmalade on top of each mousse. Top each portion with 2 teaspoons almonds. Serve immediately.

Indian Yogurt Pudding *with* Saffron, Cardamom & Toasted Nuts

(*Shrikhand*)

SERVES 4

3 cups plain drained yogurt (page 22)
or Greek yogurt (not nonfat)

2 tablespoons milk

Pinch of saffron threads (about 10 threads)

¼ cup plus 2 tablespoons sugar

Pinch of ground cardamom

Pinch of cinnamon

Pinch of freshly grated nutmeg

TOASTED NUT TOPPING

2 tablespoons unsweetened
shredded coconut

2 tablespoons sliced almonds

2 tablespoons pistachios

I learned about this luscious Indian dessert from Pankaj Uttarwar, the quality-assurance manager for Straus Family Creamery in Petaluma, California. Pankaj, a native of India, brought some of his homemade *shrikhand* to work one day, and his colleagues are still talking about it. Made from extra-thick yogurt whisked with sugar, saffron, and spices, *shrikhand* takes no skill to prepare. However, you need to allow several hours for draining the yogurt because even Greek yogurt is not thick enough. Flavor to your taste, but I think *shrikhand* is best when the spices just whisper.

Put the yogurt in a wide cheesecloth-lined sieve set over a bowl. Cover, refrigerate, and let drain for several hours until you have 2 cups of very thick yogurt. You can speed the process a little by occasionally using a rubber spatula to lift and turn the yogurt.

Put the milk and the saffron in a small saucepan or butter warmer and place over low heat until the milk is hot but not simmering. Cover and set aside to steep for 1 hour.

Put the drained yogurt in a bowl with the sugar, cardamom, cinnamon, and nutmeg. Whisk well to dissolve the sugar. Add the saffron milk ½ teaspoon at a time, whisking it in and tasting as you go. You will probably need only about 1 teaspoon; the saffron flavor should be subtle and it will bloom as the dessert chills. (Reserve any remaining saffron milk for cooking rice.) Cover the yogurt and chill thoroughly for up to 1 day.

To make the topping: Preheat the oven to 325°F. Place the coconut, almonds, and pistachios in three separate pie tins. Place in the oven. Bake the coconut until golden, about 4 minutes, stirring partway through so it toasts evenly; do not allow it to become dark brown or it will be bitter. Bake the almonds until golden brown, stirring once so they cook evenly, about 5 minutes. Bake the pistachios until fragrant, 5 to 7 minutes. Remove each from the oven as it is done and let cool. Coarsely chop the pistachios. Combine the cooled ingredients in a small bowl.

To serve, divide the pudding among 4 Martini glasses or other serving glasses. Garnish with the topping, dividing it equally. Serve immediately.

Greek Yogurt Panna Cotta *with* Strawberry-Rhubarb Sauce

SERVES 6

STRAWBERRY-RHUBARB SAUCE

¼ pound rhubarb, cut into ½-inch slices

¼ cup sugar

1 tablespoon fresh orange juice

1 cup hulled and sliced strawberries
(about 6 ounces), plus a few more for garnish

PANNA COTTA

1 cup whole milk

1-inch piece vanilla bean, split lengthwise

2 cups plain drained whole-milk yogurt
(page 22) or Greek whole-milk yogurt

¼ cup plus 2 tablespoons sugar

Pinch of kosher or sea salt

1¼ teaspoons powdered unflavored gelatin

I like to serve this panna cotta parfait-style, in clear glasses, with the ruby-red fruit puree on the bottom. Diners plunge their spoon down through the creamy layer and bring up a smidgen of sauce with each spoonful, no inverting required. However, you can also prepare the panna cotta in conventional ramekins without the sauce, unmold them at serving time, and then spoon the sauce around them. I've described both methods. Either way, you'll have a little sauce left over, just enough to enjoy with yogurt the following day.

Note that the recipe doesn't use an entire package of gelatin. The peculiar measurement I have recommended yields just the right consistency: not too stiff, not too soft. You can make the sauce and the panna cotta a day ahead, but I find the panna cotta's texture most luscious the day it is made.

To make the sauce: Put the rhubarb, sugar, and orange juice in a saucepan. Bring to a simmer over medium heat, stirring to dissolve the sugar. Cover and reduce the heat to low. Simmer gently until the rhubarb has softened completely, about 10 minutes. Watch carefully, as the mixture wants to boil up and over. Stir in the strawberries and cook, uncovered, stirring often, until they soften slightly, about 2 minutes. Puree the mixture in a food processor or blender. Refrigerate, covered, until chilled.

To make the panna cotta: Put the milk in a small saucepan. Using the tip of a paring knife, scrape the vanilla bean seeds into the milk, and then add the pod to the milk as well. Bring to a simmer over medium heat. Cover, remove from the heat, and let steep for 30 minutes. Remove the vanilla bean pod.

In another bowl, whisk together the yogurt, sugar, and salt.

Sprinkle the gelatin over the warm milk mixture and let soften for 5 minutes. Return the saucepan to medium heat and bring the milk to a simmer, whisking constantly until the gelatin completely dissolves. Cool for 5 minutes, and then whisk the milk mixture into the yogurt mixture.

continued

If you prefer to serve from glasses, parfait-style: Spoon about 2 tablespoons of the strawberry-rhubarb sauce into the bottom of each of six 6- to 8-ounce glasses. Divide the yogurt mixture equally among the glasses. (I put the yogurt mixture in a measuring cup with a pour spout so I can distribute it easily.) Cover the glasses with plastic wrap and refrigerate until set, at least 3 hours. Garnish each glass with a fresh sliced berry, if desired.

If you prefer to serve unmolded on a plate: Lightly grease six 6- to 8-ounce ramekins with vegetable oil. Divide the yogurt mixture equally among the ramekins. Set the ramekins on a tray and cover with plastic wrap or another tray. Refrigerate until set, at least 3 hours. To unmold, run a thin knife around the perimeter of each panna cotta. Place an inverted serving plate on top. Grasping the plate and ramekin with both hands, invert them and give a little shake. The panna cotta should slip out. Spoon 2 tablespoons of the strawberry-rhubarb sauce around each panna cotta, garnish with fresh berries and a mint sprig, if desired, and serve immediately.

Yogurt *with* Raspberries & Pomegranates

SERVES 4

1 large, heavy pomegranate, yielding about 1 cup of arils

½ pint (6 ounces) fresh raspberries

2 tablespoons plus 2 teaspoons superfine sugar

2 cups plain drained yogurt (page 22)

You can buy ready-to-eat pomegranate arils (that's the word for those fleshy red pearls inside), or you can extract them yourself from fresh fruit using the method I describe in the recipe. It takes so little time, and you will get juicier, tastier arils from a just-cracked pomegranate. Make this dish in fall, in the brief period when pomegranates and raspberries overlap. The best pomegranates feel heavy for their size and may even have a few cracks, signs that they're mature and juicy.

Using a paring knife, slice off the ends of the pomegranate, taking care not to cut into the juicy fruit sacs. Cut four "pole to pole" equidistant slits in the skin, slicing just skin deep so you don't pierce the arils. Put a bowl in the sink. Using both hands, crack open the pomegranate over the bowl; it should split easily into quarters where you made the slits. Working with one quarter at a time, cradle it skin side up in the fingers of one hand. Hold it over the bowl. Using the back of a wooden spoon, smack the pomegranate several times to release the arils. You may have to pry a few recalcitrant arils loose with your fingers, but most will fall between your fingers into the bowl. Repeat with the remaining quarters, and then fish out any bits of white pulp in the bowl. Measure 1 cup of arils for the recipe and reserve the rest for a snack.

Put the arils and the raspberries in a bowl and sprinkle with the sugar. Using a rubber spatula, stir gently until the sugar dissolves. Let stand for 10 minutes to draw out the juices.

Divide the yogurt among 4 Martini glasses or compote dishes. Top with the fruit and any juices, dividing them equally. Serve immediately.

Greek Yogurt Sorbet

SERVES 6

4 cups whole-milk Greek yogurt

¾ cup granulated sugar

¼ cup light corn syrup

2 tablespoons light brown sugar,
sieved to eliminate lumps

1½ teaspoons vanilla extract

¼ teaspoon kosher salt

When sweetened and churned in an ice-cream maker, Greek yogurt tastes like lemon cheesecake. Serve it with summer fruits, fresh or cooked; with fruit pies, cobblers, and crisps; or blanketed with a warm fruit sauce. I love it with fresh apricots or peaches dotted with butter and brown sugar, then broiled until they begin to caramelize. And with or without the fruit, a drizzle of honey never hurts.

In a bowl, whisk together all the ingredients. Chill well, and then freeze in an ice-cream maker according to the manufacturer's directions. Transfer to a lidded storage container, cover, and freeze for at least 1 hour to firm.

At serving time, remove the sorbet from the freezer. If it is hard or icy, let stand at room temperature until soft enough to scoop. Put a generous scoop in each of 6 serving dishes.

Absinthe's Golden Yogurt Cake

MAKES ONE 9-INCH CAKE

1½ cups sifted all-purpose flour

2½ teaspoons baking powder

1 cup plain whole-milk yogurt

½ cup vegetable oil

1½ teaspoons grated lemon, Meyer lemon, or orange zest, or a combination

¾ teaspoon vanilla extract

⅜ teaspoon kosher or sea salt

3 large eggs

1¼ cups sugar

YOGURT CREAM (OPTIONAL)

1 cup plain drained yogurt (page 22) or Greek yogurt (not nonfat)

¼ cup honey

½ teaspoon vanilla extract

1 cup heavy cream, whipped to firm peaks

This moist, simple cake has a tender golden crumb and a subtle citrus flavor. I love a thin slice—okay, a thick slice—in the middle of the afternoon with coffee, but it's also well matched with summer berries and stone fruits. My husband enjoys it for breakfast. Accompany the cake and fruit with a dollop of the Yogurt Cream, if you like. In winter, pair the cake with a citrus compote or poached quince.

This recipe is adapted from one given to me by Bill Corbett, executive pastry chef for the Absinthe Group in San Francisco, who uses yogurt frequently in his desserts. The cake stays moist for a week if stored in a lidded plastic cake container.

Preheat an oven to 350°F. Butter the bottom and sides of a 9-inch round cake pan with 2-inch sides. Line the bottom with parchment paper and dust the sides with flour, shaking out the excess.

Sift together the flour and baking powder in a bowl.

In a bowl, whisk together the yogurt, oil, zest, vanilla, and salt.

In a stand mixer fitted with a whip, beat the eggs on medium speed until frothy and well blended. Add the sugar gradually. Raise the speed to medium-high and whip until the sugar dissolves and the mixture is thick and pale, stopping the machine to scrape down the sides of the bowl at least once. Lower the mixer speed and add the yogurt mixture gradually. Add the dry ingredients gradually and beat just until well blended.

Pour the batter into the prepared cake pan, spreading it evenly. Bake on a center rack until the surface is golden brown and firm to the touch and a toothpick comes out clean, about 40 minutes. Cool on a rack for 10 minutes, and then unmold and finish cooling, top side up, on the rack.

To make the yogurt cream: In a bowl, whisk together the yogurt, honey, and vanilla. Gently fold in the whipped cream.

Slice the cake into wedges to serve, topping each portion with a dollop of the yogurt cream, if desired.

Beverages

Thinned with cold water or ice, yogurt makes a thirst-quenching refreshment. Turkish people know the drink as *ayran* (page 131), which is practically the national beverage. India's savory lassi, a cooling accompaniment to spicy meals, is prepared with yogurt, mint, ice, and salt; sweet lassi, such as the pineapple version on page 126, makes a wholesome breakfast beverage or midmorning snack. Yogurt smoothies are typically a little thicker, with creamy body from frozen bananas. With the smoothie recipes and suggestions in this chapter, you can transform fruit and yogurt into quick, nutritious, and satisfying lunches.

Fresh Pineapple Lassi

SERVES 1

¾ cup diced fresh pineapple,
preferably chilled

½ cup plain drained yogurt (page 22)
or Greek yogurt

1 tablespoon sugar

1 thin slice peeled fresh ginger,
about ¼ inch thick

2 ice cubes

Ripe fresh pineapple makes an irresistible lassi, with creamy body, bracing acidity, and natural sweetness. A quarter-size coin of fresh ginger gives it a kick. If you have the pineapple already prepped in the fridge, this lassi takes all of two minutes. No more excuses for skipping breakfast or not having time for a healthful lunch. Add a slice of whole-grain toast with peanut butter and you're fueled for hours.

Put all the ingredients in a blender and blend until the drink is smooth and frothy and you can no longer hear the rattling of the ice. Pour into a glass and serve immediately.

Strawberry-Mango Smoothie

SERVES 1 OR 2 (ABOUT 1¾ CUPS)

1 cup plain yogurt

½ cup hulled and quartered strawberries

¼ large ripe mango, sliced

½ frozen banana, peeled and cut into
2 or 3 chunks

1 tablespoon sugar

⅛ teaspoon vanilla extract

1 ice cube

VARIATION: Substitute raspberries
for the strawberries and peaches or
nectarines for the mango.

This is my favorite smoothie for late spring and early summer, when these two fruits are both at their peak. Isn't nature clever? Look for strawberries that are red all over—no white shoulders—and mangoes with a come-hither fragrance. The frozen banana adds body and a touch more tropical flavor, but it largely remains in the background.

Put the yogurt in the blender first, and then add the remaining ingredients. Blend until you can no longer hear the rattling of the ice, and pour into a tall glass.

Banana-Fig Smoothie

**SERVES 1
(ABOUT 1½ CUPS)**

4 dried figs, stems removed

1 cup plain yogurt

½ frozen banana, peeled and cut into
2 or 3 chunks

⅛ teaspoon vanilla extract

2 teaspoons sugar, or more to taste

2 ice cubes

VARIATIONS: Replace the figs with
6 whole Turkish dried apricots plumped
in hot water; add a pinch of ground
ginger. Or replace the figs with 5 large
pitted prunes; add a pinch of
ground cinnamon.

In winter, when the market offers fewer fresh fruits suitable for blending, think about dried fruit. Dried figs, prunes, peaches, and dates are delicious in a smoothie, contributing body, fiber, and natural sweetness. I plump most dried fruits in warm or hot water first, but dates are soft enough to blend without soaking.

Put the figs in a small bowl and add enough hot water to barely cover. Let stand until soft, about 1 hour. Drain, reserving the liquid. Quarter the figs.

Put the yogurt in a blender and add the figs, banana, vanilla, sugar, and ice cubes. Blend until the drink is smooth and you can no longer hear the rattling of the ice. Taste and add more sugar if desired. If the smoothie is too thick for your taste, thin with some of the reserved fig-soaking liquid. Blend again and serve immediately.

Ayran

SERVES 1
(ABOUT 1 CUP)

½ cup plain drained yogurt (page 22)
or Greek yogurt

About ½ cup spring water or
sparkling water

Kosher or sea salt

Ice cubes

Mint sprig (optional)

A refreshing yogurt beverage that Turks consume as avidly as Americans drink soda, *ayran* hardly merits a recipe. Whether made in a blender or whisked by hand, it is roughly equal parts yogurt and water, with salt to taste. It can be blended with ice or poured over ice. I recall having it on a hot day in Istanbul at a modest restaurant that specialized in pit-roasted lamb. The cook began before dawn so the meat could be served at noon, with hot flatbread, pepper relish, and icy *ayran*.

Despite *ayran*'s apparent simplicity, variations abound. According to my Turkish friend, Jale Boga Robertson, some make the beverage with sparkling water; some add mint or garlic. In cities, it is typically made with cow's-milk yogurt; in villages, with goat yogurt. The thickness depends on the preferences of the maker, but it is closer to buttermilk than to a smoothie. In the village of Susurluk, famous for its *ayran*, vendors keep the beverage in a dispenser with a pump, like the circulating soda machines at the movie theater, to make it extra foamy. Turkish schoolchildren drink *ayran* with their cafeteria lunch.

Turks are obsessed with *ayran*, Robertson told me. They turn to it for every little ailment—when they are feeling a little faint and need the salt, or when they have an upset stomach. It's not uncommon to spot Turkish men with an "*ayran* mustache." As fond as Turks are of their *ayran*, many bristled when Prime Minister Tayyip Erdogan, who disapproves of alcohol, declared it Turkey's national drink. To secular Turks, *rakı*, the potent aniseed spirit, deserves that label.

Put the yogurt in a glass and whisk in just enough water to make a beverage the consistency of buttermilk. The amount of water needed will depend on the thickness of the yogurt, but equal parts yogurt and water is about right. Whisk in salt to taste. Fill the glass with ice cubes and garnish with mint.

Alternatively, you can make *ayran* in a blender if you want it frothier. Put the yogurt in the blender and add the water, a pinch of salt, and 1 ice cube. Blend until you no longer hear the ice rattling. If the *ayran* is still too thick, add a little more water or another ice cube and blend again. Serve in a glass and garnish with mint.

Four Seasons of Fruit Smoothies

At least once a week, I whip up a smoothie for lunch, improvising with the fruit I have on hand. It's a fast-food meal that I can feel good about eating, and it can be different every time. Frozen bananas are de rigueur—I keep a stash of bananas in the freezer year-round. Because they're harder to peel when frozen, I peel them when ripe, cut them into large chunks, and pack them in quart-size freezer bags. For each smoothie, I take out only as many chunks as I need. Other fruit follows the season: berries and stone fruits in summer; persimmons in fall; kiwifruit, dried fruit, or home-canned peaches in winter; pineapple and mangoes in spring.

Hachiya persimmons, with their jelly-like texture, make exceptionally creamy smoothies. Let the fruits ripen fully at room temperature—they should feel squishy all over—and then toss them whole into the freezer. As needed, take one out, run under cold water to soften slightly, cut out the leafy cap, and quarter the fruit with a chef's knife (careful—it will be hard and slippery). Use alone in a smoothie or mix with banana.

Here are a few tips for making yogurt smoothies:

- Save calories by using nonfat or low-fat yogurt. I prefer whole-milk yogurt in almost every other instance, but in smoothies, I don't miss the fat.

- Most smoothies need some sweetening. Granulated sugar always works, but for variety, try brown sugar, maple sugar, maple syrup, honey, agave nectar, date sugar, or fruit preserves. Fruits vary in acidity and sugar content, so it's difficult to predict how much sweetener you will need. Start with a small amount—perhaps 1 teaspoon granulated sugar per ½ cup yogurt. You can always add more after you blend and taste.

- For easier blending, put the yogurt and any liquid ingredients, such as orange juice, in the blender before the frozen ingredients.

- If you make a lot of smoothies, keep a bag of crushed ice in the freezer. Crushed ice blends more readily than ice cubes.

- Need more protein in your meals? Add a spoonful of peanut butter or almond butter to your smoothie.

Bibliography

The following books and publications were helpful to me in preparing this manuscript.

Algar, Ayla. *Classical Turkish Cooking.* New York: HarperCollins, 1991.

Batmanglij, Najmieh. *New Food of Life: Ancient Persian and Modern Iranian Cooking and Ceremonies.* Washington, DC: Mage Publishers, 1994.

———. *Persian Cooking for a Healthy Kitchen.* Washington, DC: Mage Publishers, 1994.

Crocker, Pat. *The Yogurt Bible.* Toronto: Robert Rose, 2010.

Davidson, Alan, ed. *The Oxford Companion to Food.* Oxford: Oxford University Press, 1999.

Der Haroutunian, Arto. *The Yogurt Cookbook.* London: Grub Street, 2010.

Hansen, Eric. "Of Yogurt and Yörüks." *Saudi Aramco World* 59, no. 4 (July–August 2008).

Helou, Anissa. *Lebanese Cuisine.* New York: St. Martin's Griffin, 1994.

Kahate, Ruta. *5 Spices, 50 Dishes.* San Francisco: Chronicle Books, 2007.

Kochilas, Diane. *The Glorious Foods of Greece.* New York: William Morrow, 2001.

Kremezi, Aglaia. *The Foods of the Greek Islands.* New York: Houghton Mifflin, 2000.

McGee, Harold. *On Food and Cooking: The Science and Lore of the Kitchen.* New York: Scribner, 2004.

Mendelson, Anne. *Milk: The Surprising Story of Milk Through the Ages.* New York: Alfred A. Knopf, 2008.

Roden, Claudia. *The New Book of Middle Eastern Food.* New York: Alfred A. Knopf, 2000.

Sahni, Julie. *Classic Indian Cooking.* New York: William Morrow, 1980.

Sortun, Ana. *Spice: Flavors of the Eastern Mediterranean.* New York: Regan Books, 2006.

Uvezian, Sonia. *The Book of Yogurt.* New York: HarperCollins, 1978.

Wolfert, Paula. *The Cooking of the Eastern Mediterranean.* New York: HarperCollins, 1994.

Wright, Clifford A. *A Mediterranean Feast.* New York: William Morrow, 1999.

Yogurt: A Where Healthy Food Starts Guide. Sioux Falls: Cultures for Health, 2013.

Resources

SPICES AND SEASONINGS

ALEPPO OR MARAŞ PEPPER, *DUKKA, VADOUVAN,* AND *ZA'ATAR*

Kalustyan's
123 Lexington Ave.
New York, NY 10016
212-685-3451
www.kalustyans.com

Maraş pepper is identified as Maras Biber on the company's website.

The Spice House
Multiple retail locations
847-328-3711
www.thespicehouse.com

Whole Spice Warehouse
1364 N. McDowell Blvd., Suite 20
Petaluma, CA 94954
707-778-1750

Retail:
Oxbow Public Market
610 First St.
Napa, CA 94559
www.wholespice.com

EXTRA-COARSE (NO. 4) BULGUR

Middle Eastern markets are the best source for extra-coarse (no. 4) bulgur. It is also available online from Amazon. Brands to look for include Duru (imported from Turkey), and Sahadi, SADAF, and Arisa (the last three processed by California's Sunnyland Mills). If you are buying bulgur from supermarket bulk bins, look for bulgur that is golden in color, not brown.

For more information on sourcing: www.sunnylandmills.com.

EQUIPMENT

PLYBAN CHEESECLOTH

Hoegger Supply Company
200 Providence Rd.
Fayetteville, GA 30215
800-221-4628
www.hoeggerfarmyard.com

Get Culture
501 Tasman St.
Madison, WI 53714
608-268-0462
www.getculture.com

DRY YOGURT CULTURES

Cultures for Health
1801 N. Louise Dr.
Sioux Falls, SD 57107
800-962-1959
www.culturesforhealth.com

YOGURT MAKER

Brød & Taylor Folding Proofer
P.O. Box 712
Williamstown, MA 01267
800-768-7064
413-458-9933
www.brodandtaylor.com

About the Author

Janet Fletcher is the author or coauthor of more than two dozen books on food and beverages, including *Cheese & Wine*, *Cheese & Beer*, and *The Cheese Course*. Her weekly email newsletter, *Planet Cheese*, is read by cheese enthusiasts internationally, and she is a member of the *Guilde Internationale des Fromagers*. A longtime contributor to the *San Francisco Chronicle*, Janet has received three James Beard Awards and the IACP Bert Greene Award for her newspaper journalism. Her food and beverage writing has also appeared in numerous national magazines, including *Saveur*, *Bon Appétit*, *Fine Cooking*, *Culture*, and *Food & Wine*. She lives in Napa Valley but teaches cooking and cheese-appreciation classes around the country (see www.janetfletcher.com).

Acknowledgments

I would like to acknowledge with gratitude the following people, who assisted me in preparing this book. For technical information, I am indebted to Jennifer Bice of Redwood Hill Farm and to Casey Carroll, Helen Lentze, Rich Martin, Albert Straus, and Pankaj Uttarwar of Straus Family Creamery. Haven Bourque also provided valuable assistance. Expert background on yogurt and probiotics came from Mary Ellen Sanders, PhD, of Dairy & Food Culture Technologies. The illustrious Harold McGee helped with advice on yogurt stability. Others who helped me with recipes, recipe suggestions, or recipe testing include Janice Beaman, Ed Blonz, chef Chris Borcich of Troya Restaurant, Angela Bortugno, pastry chef Bill Corbett of the Absinthe Group, Pam Elder, Anissa Helou, Sotiris Kitrilakis, Christine Maxa, Jale Boga Robertson, Betty Teller, and Paula Wolfert. Photographer Eva Kolenko, food stylist George Dolese, and prop stylist Glenn Jenkins made the book's images more beautiful than I could have imagined. Many thanks to Julie Dykstra and Brød & Taylor for the folding proofer that kept me constantly supplied with superb homemade yogurt. This book would still be just a fantasy without my incomparable agent, Carole Bidnick, who found the perfect home for my idea; and without the skill and care of editor Lisa Regul, copy editor Abigail Bok, and the entire enthusiastic team at Ten Speed Press.

Index

Copyright © 2015 by Janet Fletcher
Photographs copyright © 2015 by Eva Kolenko

All rights reserved.
Published in the United States by Ten Speed Press, an imprint
of the Crown Publishing Group, a division of Random House
LLC, a Penguin Random House Company, New York.
www.crownpublishing.com
www.tenspeed.com

Ten Speed Press and the Ten Speed Press colophon are
registered trademarks of Random House LLC.

Library of Congress Cataloging-in-Publication Data
Fletcher, Janet, 1956- author.
 Yogurt : sweet and savory recipes for breakfast, lunch, and
dinner / Janet Fletcher. — First edition.
     pages cm
1. Cooking (Yogurt) I. Title.
TX759.5.Y63F54 2015
641.6'71476—dc23
                                         2014036579

Hardcover ISBN: 978-1-60774-712-3
eBook ISBN: 978-1-60774-713-0

Printed in China

Design by Nami Kurita
Food styling by George Dolese

10 9 8 7 6 5 4 3 2 1

First Edition